HOME OPERATED BUSINESS OPPORTUNITIES FOR THE DISABLED

Compiled and Edited By
Raymond C. Cheever
Publisher and Editor, Accent On Living Magazine

Accent Special Publications
Cheever Publishing, Inc.
Post Office Box 700
Bloomington, Illinois 61701

Cheever Publishing, Inc., serves disabled persons by collecting and disseminating specialized information. Services are available through ACCENT On Living, a quarterly magazine; Accent On Information, a computerized retrieval system; and Accent Special Publications.

First Edition
First Printing, October 1977
Second Printing, April 1982

Accent Special Publications
Cheever Publishing, Inc.
P.O. Box 700, Bloomington, Illinois 61701

Printed in the United States of America

WHY THIS BOOK?

This book has been compiled as a guide to those individuals who, through illness or injury, find that the best way to make a productive living is to operate a business in their own homes. It is a book of practical, workable ideas.

It may sometimes seem too difficult or complicated to start and operate a business in one's own home. This book will attempt to reveal how others have overcome the obstacles involved.

In general, you will find that the obstacles are overcome by persistence and methodical thinking. Certainly the task is not easy, but success in any endeavor depends on a positive attitude. Your attitude alone can't guarantee success, but a poor attitude is an almost certain guarantee of failure.

Perhaps you are now trying to decide what kind of work you want to do. Consider your own skills and interests, and physical limitations which will not interfere with your work.

Actively seek information from people already in your prospective venture, especially those with disabilities similar to yours.

The people described in this book aren't telling you what to do, they are saying what can be done, what resources are available. Some may have, at one time, considered giving up, but most succeeded at what they began.

Many of these stories are taken directly from the pages of Accent on Living magazine, and are included here as a guide to what can be done.

Your local public library will prove to be an invaluable asset for information and resources. Publications in your field, and some dealing in a general nature with starting a small business, are all at your disposal at the library.

Don't jump hastily into any business deal. Few opportunities are so fleeting as to warrant hasty decisions. Look thoroughly into what you are attempting. The research will pay off in the end.

On offers of franchises and other dealings where you work for someone else, it's always wise to check with the chamber of commerce or better business bureau in the area before committing your time or money.

Whatever you do, if you do it well, you will stand a good chance of success.

NOTE: Because some of the articles range back as far as 20 years — as does ACCENT ON LIVING magazine from which they were reprinted — some of the wages and costs mentioned will be out-of-date.

CONTENTS

Money-Making Opportunities And New Job Skills Are Available To Homebound Persons Through The Mail — But, Beware

> **299—Help Wanted**
> WANTED: Housewives and other homebound persons to get bilked of nearly $500 million a year. No experience needed. Few hours a week. Send $1 for details to; P.O. Box 000, Gypsville, U.S.A.

You're not likely to see this advertisement anywhere. However, if you read between the lines of some ads promising high profits and big earnings from only a few hours work a week, assuring you of an instant guaranteed market, insisting that experience isn't necessary and requiring money to learn how to take advantage of this opportunity of a lifetime, you had better investigate before investing more than a postage stamp.

While there are many legitimate ways to make money by operating a mail order business or working part-time, there are just as many ways to be gypped by unscrupulous operators.

An advertisement which appeared in several U.S. newspapers offering women the opportunity to "Earn up to $1.68 an hour sewing baby shoes in your own home" drew more than 200,000 inquiries. Just as in most such advertisements, there was a catch in this one. The sewer had to pay a small registration fee just for an opportunity to demonstrate her skill in sewing a pair of wool-felt shoes for infants. Virtually every one of the 60,000 prospects failed to measure up to the promoter's "high" standards of craftsmanship.

Another common scheme is the ad claiming that you can make money addressing envelopes or post cards at home. You must first, however, buy the cards from the promoter and pay for the stamps yourself. You then address them and receive a commission on all sales made from your "mail campaign".

The catch, as discovered in a recent postal investigation, is that the average amount that could be earned by persons doing this at home was about 45¢ a week. One case being investigated by postal authorities this year involves the sale of a "complete starter kit" titled "Beginners Kit For Making $250 Per Thousand Stuffing Envelopes."

And there are always promises of "easy riches" from selling your products by operating your own mail order business.

One case involved a young man who decided to market an informational booklet by mail order. The initial drive to enter the field was provided by an ad with the headline reading "The Lazy Man's Way To Riches," and the specific idea came from an ad promoting selling how-to books by mail.

The young man researched and wrote a 10,000 word booklet entitled, "A Guide To Selling Your Own Home," about selling a house without using a real estate broker. He reprinted his manuscript at very little cost and obtained a copyright. He set his selling price at $2 per copy.

Using the advice in his mail order instruction manuals he composed an advertisement with a coupon, placing it on the television page of his local newspaper. The ad cost him $75 for one issue. Everything had been done by the book; a quality product, a suffi-cient markup, a clever ad and lots of faith and confidence.

The newspaper had a circulation of over 400,000. He needed only 50 orders to break even, a return of 1 of every 1,000 papers printed.

In the days following the ad a total of 8 orders came in, one of them from his sister. His investment of $100 and dozens of hours brought a return of $16. By then it was too late to return the mail order material, adding another $10 to his loss.

Another angle of the mail order racketeer is business opportunities. Franchises — while ordinarily a legitimate and fast-growing industry — are favorites of mail order swindlers.

In one case, a man falsely told prospective franchisers that they would be supplied stereo "8-track" cartridges of current musical "hits". They actually received only reproduced or out-dated recordings of little value. More than 400 investors in 30 states were swindled of an estimated $1.3 million and the promoter was convicted of mail fraud.

Another frequent rip-off is the ad offering part-time employment as operators of phoney routes for vending machines. This is often in the form of an ad in a help-wanted column.

Victims, rather than being hired to serve an established route, are often told how much more they can make by owning their own vending units. In a typical case, those expecting to earn profits of up to $30 a month per machine were lured into paying $100 each for hot-nut vending units which cost the promoter only $17. In one case, the victims' "profits" didn't even cover the expenses.

Last year two men were sentenced to prison for fraudulently selling vending machine franchises. They had swindled 34 investors out of about $127,000.

The "little guy" isn't the only one victimized by money-making schemes. One get-rich-quick deal, which received much national publicity recently, included the victimization of unsuspecting bankers, lawyers, doctors and possibly even a U.S. Senator and a Congressman.

While most mail order business opportunities probably aren't fraudulent, you should always investigate any company carefully before sending any money. Check them out through the Chamber of Commerce and Better Business Bureau in their area as well as the local offices of the Federal Trade Commission and the Postal Inspector.

Information you may find useful if considering going into a home and/or mail order business can be found in "Bibliography No. 1, Handicrafts", "Bibliography No. 2, Home Businesses" and "Bibliography No. 3, Selling By Mail Order" available from the Small Business Administration, U.S. Department of Commerce,* Washington, D.C. 20416 and "Mail Fraud Laws Protecting: consumers, investors, businessmen, patients, students" which is available for 35¢ from the Superintendent of Documents, U.S. Government Printing Office, Washington, D.C. 20402.

> **300—Home Study Schools**
>
> LEARN AT HOME: You can learn anything in the privacy of your own home and earn at least $200 a week after you graduate. Write today for details. Box 000, Gypsville, U.S.A.

The promise of an exciting, high-paying job and vastly increased abilities to earn money are the usual lures capitalized on by fake correspondence schools. Persons who are homebound are particularly susceptible to home study courses which offer the false promise that jobs in the subjects they teach — sometimes such subjects as computer programming and U.S. Civil Service — are available merely by studying the books they send you and applying for the job.

Fraudulent correspondence schools will accept almost anyone willing to sign a contract for up to $1,000.

There are, however, many legitimate home study courses which offer skills sometimes difficult to obtain any other way. These legitimate courses are operated through accredited schools and have qualified teachers who maintain a two-way communication with students as they go through the educational process of taking the course and submitting lessons.

If you want to sign up to take a home study course, first find out if: (1) the school is accredited, (2) you can afford it, (3) it is the course you really need to learn the

*Out of print. You may be able to obtain this from your local library.

skill you want.

Accreditation of private home study courses is conducted through the accrediting commission of the National Home Study Council. The Council is designated by the U.S. Department of Education to accredit private correspondence courses. You may request a free copy of the "Directory of Accredited Private Home Study Schools" from the National Home Study Council, 1601 18th Street N.W., Washington, D.C. 20009.

That a school is accredited by the National Home Study Council simply means that it meets certain standards set by professionals in the field. Those criteria include an assurance that the school has been in operation for several years; has clear-cut educational objectives, methods and testing procedures; has a qualified faculty; is honest in advertising and promotional materials; charges reasonable tuition and has a satisfactory refund policy.

If a college or university is offering the course, you should find out if it is a member of the National University Extension Association. One easy way to do this is to send $1.00* to the NUEA, One DuPont Circle, Suite 360, Washington, D.C. 20036 and ask for the "Guide to Independent Study Through Correspondence Instruction," a list of courses available through NUEA members.

Colleges and universities affiliated with the NUEA are accredited by the educational accrediting agency in their area.

*Now $2.00 + .46 postage.

That a correspondence school isn't accredited shouldn't be the sole criteria for deciding not to take the courses it offers. After all, according to the standards, even the best school couldn't be accredited for several years. Besides, maybe it offers a subject not available from accredited schools. However, investigate carefully before deciding to enroll in such a correspondence school. Check with the local Better Business Bureau and your State Department of Education and write to the U.S. Office of Education, Adult Education Section, Washington, D.C. 20202. A few letters written before you sign the contract may save you a great deal of money and trouble as well as assuring that you learn as much as possible from the course you finally take.

Whether the school is accredited or not, you should ask for names of persons in your area who have taken the course and talk with them about the school. Legitimate schools will welcome courteous investigation. They have nothing to hide. If the school or a representative tries to rush you or pressure you to sign up before you finish checking them out, that alone may be a good reason to start looking for another school.

The second thing you should consider before signing up for the course is whether or not you can afford to take it. Obtain a catalog and a written statement telling you exactly how much the course will cost, including interest on any time payments and the cost of any equipment necessary for taking the course. Also, find out if there is a cancellation clause in the contract you will have to sign and, if so, how much it will cost to cancel the contract.

Make up your mind that you will finish the course before signing up. Don't just sign up on a whim.

The third thing to find out before taking the course is whether or not it is the right one to take to learn the skill you are interested in acquiring. Contact people who hire persons with skills you want to learn and people who are presently employed in the type of job you want to train for. Some will be able to give you specific suggestions on which home study courses to take. Others will tell you that companies hiring people for that kind of job have their own training programs.

A Positive Outlook Is Important

By Myrtle Shay

Have you a handicap that causes those around you to regard you with pity? Do they say, "Poor Helen, she can't see," or "Betty will never be able to use her arms," or "Isn't it terrible that John is confined to a wheel chair? Poor fellow, he'll never walk again."?

If you are one of this group, how do you respond to such remarks? Do you let them "get you down"? Or, do you realize that people who go about expressing pity for others may be objects of pity, themselves? The person who is so thoughtless as to make another feel that his case is hopeless, is far more to be pitied than the one who has suffered the physical affliction. If the handicapped person listens to others' words of woe, he will indeed be disabled, mentally as well as physically. And the mental incapacity will be by far the worse.

When someone thoughtlessly suggests that, because another has a physical infirmity, he is beyond help; that he can never attain happiness; that he is of no use in the world, that person is not only being cruel; he is being untruthful.

The spirit that lives in us is forever working to compensate for any physical loss we suffer. Since this is true, how much better it is for us to take stock of what we have left, rather than to morbidly contemplate our loss! So many wonderful things have been accomplished by those whom others looked upon as helpless, that no one with a handicap need feel his case is hopeless.

Fannie Crosby, perhaps the greatest hymn writer of all time, lost her sight at the age of six weeks. But Fannie Crosby was determined to be happy in spite of her handicap, and in later years, she came to look upon her blindness as a blessing because, she said, it gave her the solitude in which to write her songs undisturbed by the world about her.

A few years ago, my husband and I were visiting in a city in the Southwest, when the speedometer on our car developed trouble. Someone directed us to a shop for repairs, telling us to ask for a certain man. "He's the best in his line on the West Coast," we were told. How astonished we were to find that this highly skilled young man was little more than three feet tall, because of a twisted spine. We liked him at once for his cheery smile and the way he went about his work. After our first surprise, somehow we ceased to think of him as handicapped. He seemed so competent, so full of life, so happy.

There are t h o u s a n d s of paraplegics who are earning their own living, many of them supporting families. Until he moved away last year, I had a next-door neighbor, who, because of crippling polio, is confined to a wheel chair. Nevertheless, he is steadily employed, and in his leisure moments is always willing to use his skill as an electrician to help out a neighbor. Instead of complaining, this man is busy and happy and takes great pleasure in helping others to solve their problems.

A certain woman with whom I formerly corresponded, had been confined to a wheel chair for twenty-seven years, because of a crippling form of arthritis, which rendered most of her body useless. But Mrs. L—was not idle. She had organized a local Sunshine Club for shut-ins and she operated a gift shop, selling the articles made by the handicapped. She did beautiful typing, in spite of the fact that most of her fingers were useless.

"At first, I was filled with despair," she wrote me. "I brooded over my misfortune and was angry and resentful. 'Why had God let this happen to me? Why should I be singled out for such undeserved punishment?' I asked. But gradually I came to realize that fretting and feeling sorry for myself would get me nowhere and I began to look around for work that I could do; for work that would help other hopeless shut-ins, like myself, to find renewed interest in life. I obtained the names of other handicapped persons and wrote them, asking what they wanted most of all besides health. Their answers were all the same: 'Work!' Something they could do to help earn their livelihood and keep their minds off of their troubles."

So Mrs. L—, out of her own limited resources, rented a small store on a busy thoroughfare, and stocked it with articles made by these handicapped people. There were gorgeously dressed dolls, crocheted p i e c e s, beautifully embroidered linens, baby clothes, ornaments, etc. The shop was a success from the start and Mrs. L— was very happy waiting on her customers from her wheel chair.

Once she wrote: "Except for my affliction, I might never have known the comfort that faith can give. Because there was no other place to go, I turned to the Almighty. In my despair, I reached for God, touched Him, and was startled to find Him alive."

Are we, with all our health, more fortunate than this courageous shut-in? Are we happier? I doubt it. How many of us have touched God and found Him alive?

A very lovely girl, who was a polio victim, confined to a wheel chair, wrote me some years ago that she was sure she was happier than she ever could have been had she lived a normal life. "I can truly say,," she wrote, "although it may sound fantastic, that my physical disability has enabled me to live a fuller, richer life than I would have otherwise. It has given me so much, it is difficult to explain. Sometimes we are prone to dash about in our own little world, with our own little circle of friends and pay little attention to others. I wonder if I might not have been this type of person. I feel my handicap has given me a better understanding, not only of myself, but of others. I have a better sense of values. I've made many friends I would not have known otherwise—all over the world and in every walk of life. It has given me the desire to help others less fortunate. Under the circumstances, I can have no regrets."

Like Mrs. L—, this girl learned the joy of helping others. Many handicapped persons are indebted to her for a renewal of their happiness. At the time of our correspondence, she was making and selling wire jewelry. She was also teaching others and helping them to find a market for their product. I am sure she too, is loved by many she has never met.

It seems that when one loses some physical power, God steps in and replaces it with unlimited spiritual force. Those who are seriously handicapped must have an outlet for the energy that is in them. Failing to find it through physical means, they turn to the spiritual.

In truth, spirit is the reality and the physical body, the unreality, the transient part of us. So, those who grow in spirit are putting on more of the reality of life and letting go of the tangible, passing things that are as nothing in the sight of God. "It is the spirit that quickeneth; the flesh profiteth nothing." The handicapped are daily demonstrating this great truth.

Dear Friend, if you are a so-called handicapped person, waste no time in self-pity or gloomy thoughts. Many of your number are far richer in the things of the spirit than we who are physically whole. And only the things of the spirit can make us truly happy, for they do not fade with time nor lose their brightness when we use them much.

Love and faith and joy are of

the spirit and he, who has these three, is rich, though his body be wasted away. You, who are handicapped, remember that always. And, remembering, lift up your hearts in thankfulness for the spirit within you; the spirit that giveth life; the spirit that cannot be conquered; the Spirit of God, Himself.

The flame of life that burns in each of us is unquenchable. It cannot be destroyed, for it is God. For every physical defect we have, spirit will compensate us a hundred fold, if we will let it. If we turn our thoughts to God and let His will be done through us, like Mrs. L—and the others I have mentioned, we can live successful, happy lives in spite of handicaps.

These folks are symbols of triumphant living. Considering what they have done, who can say that they have not been successful? And who can doubt but that God does have a place for each and every one of us regardless of handicaps and that He will help us find it if we ask Him.

There are many Mrs. L—'s in the world; many with faith and courage as deep and abiding as hers. Their bodies may be bound to wheel chairs, but their spirits roam the Kingdom of the Stars.

Ten Points To Help You Identify Competent Trade Schools

Learning a new job? A very practical and valuable way for you to (1) become trained so that you can get and hold a particular job or (2) become trained so that you can become qualified to hold a better job at a higher wage, is to enroll in a home correspondence course or attend a "qualified" trade school where you will be trained for the particular type of work you are interested in doing.

Be careful though! Before you go ahead with a school, there are some things you should check first. You will want to know how well —or how poorly—the school is doing its job and your only guide will be your own personal evaluation.

These ten points should help you to make a sound decision:

1. See how much and what kind of equipment the school has on its premises. See if the students are permitted to use it—how often —and for how long. How does the equipment compare with that which the student will be using after he completes his training?

2. Check on the background of the school's instructors. Have they had solid, practical experience—or are they reading the lesson right out of the book? Are there enough instructors to give the students a reasonable amount of personal at-

tention? If you are in some doubt, try to find out where the instructor is working—or has worked—and call his employer to check his qualifications.

3. Contact the employment managers of various local companies. See what they think of the school. If you don't know any such companies, see which ones are advertising for help in the classified pages of the local newspapers and call them.

4. Ask the school for a list of its past students. Call them and ask them what they think of the school. Would they recommend it? Did it help them get a job? Don't settle for one or two opinions; call a dozen—and pick them at random.

5. Find out what teaching aids, manuals, textbooks, etc., the school is using. Do they seem adequate? Do classes meet regularly and follow an established course outline?

6. Check the Better Business Bureau. It will not recommend, but it will provide you with lists of schools from which to choose. It

will not advise, but it will provide information. If complaints have been received about certain schools, this information will be in their files.

7. Visit all of the schools available. Compare one against the other as to equipment, instructors, course outline, etc. The Better Business Bureau's list of schools will help you in reaching them all.

8. Beware of high-pressure salesmen. Don't be talked into anything; make up your own mind. Don't listen to extravagant promises.

9. Know what you're signing. Don't rely on oral promises. Schools are responsible only to do what they have agreed to do in writing.

10. Beware of the promise of "guaranteed" placement. No one can promise that he's going to get you a job and none of the legitimate schools will make such a promise. The school should make an attempt to place its students, however, and its percentage of success should be a good indication of how good the school is.

Business Loans For The Handicapped

Would you like to own and manage your own private business? Disabled persons who are capable of starting their own business operation should be aware of the help available from the Small Business

Administration, which administers loans under Title IV of the Economic Opportunity Act of 1964, which authorizes the making or guaranteeing of loans to help in setting up or strengthening small businesses.

When considering your own business, don't overlook the services of another agency, the Vocational Rehabilitation Administration whose primary work is restoring handicapped people to employment.

These two agencies, the SBA and the VRA, have just announced a program where they will be able to work closely together to help disabled persons establish their own business enterprises. Meetings are now being arranged and held where full details of the SBA loan programs are being provided to rehabilitation counselors. The primary purpose of this joint program is to bring together the experience and resources of these two public agencies, in order to make better use of these small loan programs in the rehabilitation field.

Could You Make A Go Of It?

It is important that you consider the answer to this question carefully and thoroughly. It should be emphasized that all handicapped people are not necessarily suitable candidates for opportunities in the business arena. Not only is there the factor of whether or not you have the ability to be successful, that is the necessary knowledge, but there is the all-important factor of whether or not you would be happy in your own business. You can get help in assessing your own abilities and aptitudes by talking to experienced and successful businessmen. The counselor in your area representing the VRA can be extremely helpful to you.

In Summary

If you want to consider the chances of your being successful in your own small business, proceed at once to get as much information and as many facts as possible from as many sources as possible. Then spend some thinking time, reading and rereading all the information you have gathered, and the notes you have made.

Then—and this is important—make your *own* decision on what you want to do! Work hard and don't give up—you may have started a whole new life for yourself.

Some Disabled Eligible For Small Business Loans

The Small Business Administration (SBA) Act Amendments of 1972 provide for loans for nonprofit organizations for the handicapped or loans to handicapped individuals.

The loans may be used by any handicapped person to establish, acquire or operate a small business.

For information, contact your local or regional SBA office.

Steps In Starting Your Own Business

Home operated businesses by the physically handicapped has always been a subject of great interest to the editor of ACCENT On Living magazine. There are many different types of successful small businesses. Successful because there is always a need for a special service, a different or better way of doing something, and for new products, new designs or better ways of meeting the needs and demands of the people all around us who buy.

However, everybody is not qualified to operate their own small business. You should be a hardy person and like to work for yourself, you have to like people and be willing to do things—to serve, in the full sense of the word. You must "go after business" by being aggressive without being antagonistic, and you must be ambitious.

Seven Basic Rules

1. Analyze yourself—what is your education, do you have any special training, what are your hobbies and what are your physical abilities (strength, range of motion, ability to move, etc.).

2. Get information—(see list at end of article.), get as much as you can pertaining to your special interests and everything that contains some information on starting a small business. Types of informa-

tion are: licensing laws, opportunities, location, financing, organization, accounting and bookkeeping, taxation, advertising, trade associations, selling by mail, etc.

3. Make a decision—as to what business you want to go into based on all the information you will then have at your command.

4. Get organized—get everything you need to do business and start slowly but steadily with your emphasis always on quality and service.

5. Look like you are in business—keep your shop or office clean and neat—everything in its place. Have business stationery printed at a good local printer.

6. Work hard—follow the things you learned in step 2 above.

7. Keep alert—always to new ideas for your business.

Available From The Superintendent Of Public Documents, Government Printing Office, Washington, D. C.

"Starting and Managing a Small Business of Your Own"—40c. Includes seven chapters: 'So You Are Thinking of Going Into Business'; 'Starting A New Business'; 'Buying a Going Business'; 'Managing Your Business'; 'Looking into Special Requirements'; 'Checklist For Starting a Business'; and 'Keeping

Up to Date'. Discusses the types of business a prospective businessman should choose, the chances of success, return on investments, where to locate, how much capital is needed and where to get the money, what a small businessman should know about buying and pricing, problems in selecting and training personnel, laws and regulations a business will be subjected to, and types of insurance and taxes.

"Small Business Enterprises for the Severely Handicapped"—45c. A catalog of small business experiences of the homebound and severely handicapped in the state-federal vocational rehabilitation program.

"How Trade Associations Help Small Business". Small Business Administration Annual number 2. Price 55c.*

Available from the Small Business Administration, Washington, D. C.

"Selling By Mail With Limited Capital"—no charge.* The popularity of success stories about selling by mail has created the impression that selling through the mail from one's home is a simple, easy method of earning a living, or of substantially supplementing one's income in spare time. Contrary to the many glowing descriptions of opportunities in mail-order selling by writers, promoters, and planned sellers, there are many pitfalls for beginners. Success in mail selling calls for study, experience, capital, organizing ability and courage in meeting reverses.

"Handicrafts and Home Products for Profit"—*—no charge. This reference is for the use of people who have attained a degree of expertness in some craft or skill and would like to build a business based on it. Woodworking, textile art, metal arts, small animal raising, and cooking are among the many pursuits carried on around the home that sometimes become the nucleus for a successful business enterprise.

Available from other sources

"Adventures in Small Business: 119 Success Stories of ideas, products and inventions that have developed into profit-making business", by the editors of Fortune-Time, Inc., New York; McGraw-Hill, 1957, pp. 273, price $3.75.* These stories indicate that the entrepreneur is still a hardy breed, . . . it seems evident that if he has a good product or an idea and the energy to develop it, he can create a successful business.

"Eleven Ways You Can Raise Money", by J. K. Lasser, Nation's Business Magazine, June 1950 issue. pp. 32. Here are some methods of raising money for a new business—from friends and their relative's friends, your bank, use of business opportunities ads, risk capital, Small Business Administration, insurance companies, creditors, through aid of lawyers and C.P.A.'s, etc.

*These publications are now out of print and may be available from your public library. McGraw Hill has suggested "How To Start And Manage Your Own Business", which they do have in print now, may be useful.

A Job In Your Home

Research project uncovers actual job opportunities that could be opened up across the country to handicapped who are homebound.

It's a fair estimate that some two million disabled people in the United States today are homebound and that only a small handful are employed in any way.

In addition to the physical problems, architectural barriers and the problems of transportation prevent many handicapped individuals from getting to a job. Consequently, their lives and ability or potential ability are wasted.

The Human Resources Center, Henry Viscardi, Jr., President, has just completed a pilot project designed to explore and develop job opportunities which could be performed gainfully by someone at home.

Viscardi said, "Our results show that not only were jobs available and there were homebound people who could be successfully placed, but that these occupations could be developed regionally and across the nation. We have also determined that these excellent career opportunities are greatly rewarding to the homebound individual."

He went on to say, "We hope that our findings will stimulate others to explore the challenge and dedicate their efforts to bring lives of meaning to the severely disabled homebound of our country."

This project has revealed, possibly for the first time in an organized way, that new vocational opportunities for the severely disabled homebound *can* be developed and vocational placements can assist these people in returning to productive lives. Industries *can* economically hire the homebound *if* the jobs are carefully selected and *if* an interested agency is available to assist in evaluation and training.

There is much equipment available on the market today which the severely disabled can utilize in performing jobs with few, if any, modifications.

Henry Albert is a cardiac working at home as a tele-service claims agent for Insurance Company of North America.

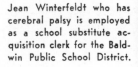

Mrs. Lillian Riffel works as a bank credit collection clerk at Franklin National Bank despite her inability to ambulate due to an osteorthritic hip.

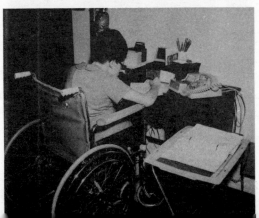

Jean Winterfeldt who has cerebral palsy is employed as a school substitute ac-quisition clerk for the Bald-win Public School District.

Make Money At Home Opportunities: Friend Or Fraud?

by Alan R. Logan

If you are bedbound, homebound, unable to get or hold steady jobs because of a disability, or now employed but uncertain of your future, you have undoubtedly eyed with curiosity and some hope the myriad of advertisements offering opportunities to make money working at home. These ads appear in local newspapers, nationally circulated "Big City" newspapers, in the mechanics magazines, in home and garden magazines, and in just about all publications featuring a classified ad department. They are aimed at the housewife who wishes to supplement her budget, the dissatisfied worker who feels that his regular income is inadequate, the idealist who envisions himself as the head of his very own corporation, the aged, and the infirm. Some cautiously offer "Extra Cash, full or part-time work, in your own home". Others boastfully promise "$9.00/hour in your own home business or YOU can earn $50 to $900 per month and be your own boss"!

Should you undertake to answer one or more of these "come-ons" you will be venturing out into the great unknown and unless you carry with you the necessary equipment (caution, analysis, and investigation) you will, more than likely, become one of the many millions of unwary "suckers" who annually pour over one-half a billion dollars into the pockets of the "Mail Order Moguls". To personally investigate each and every "pitch" could very easily consume a year of your time and hundreds of dollars. Since many are ligitimate and rewarding, how best then can you separate the chaff from the grain?

There are, basically, eight catagories of "Home Business" offers. You cannot, usually, determine from the wording of the ad into which pit you are likely to fall. The best course then is to invest in a few dollars worth of postal cards, inquire, await replies, and then classify them. If they fall into any of the first six classes, invest no further. If they are of the nature of the latter two, seek more info and advice before plunging in. They really legit ones will gladly supply you with all the information that you seek, free of charge. They will volunteer Dunn & Bradstreet ratings and bank references. They will make no bold claims of sure profits but will present all details clearly and sincerely state that results are strictly up to you. All sales material and/or necessary equipment will be supplied to you either free of charge or at cost. The prime rule to follow should be: If the company will trust you with the information expensive sales promotion literature, and selling kits (postpaid) then they are earnestly and honestly seeking your help in presenting their product or have a worthwhile product to sell you that you can use to set yourself up in your own business.

Catagorically, these are the eight types of plans, schemes, or opportunities: 1. The sellers of "Inside Information", instruction courses, agency promotion of your work (unknown literary agents, song pluggers, etc.), sellers of lists of product source or market at exceptionally high cost (info of this nature is readily available from your nearest library).

Alan Logan operates Logan Enterprises from his home.

2. Sellers of plans, formulas, unfinished products, breeding animals, or equipment that offer to buy back, from you, the finished product if it is up to their standards (It never will be).

3. Sellers of plans, formulas, unfinished products, breeding animals, or equipment that guarantee to put you in touch with a ready and willing market. In either group 2 or 3, if the idea or product were a surefire seller they wouldn't think of letting millions of outsiders in on it. They originate an idea and when it is no longer a big money maker they profit by selling the overworked plan to others.

4. Sellers of professional advertising skill and know-how who charge exorbitant fees to prepare ads and sales letters for the *certain* promotion of your own product or service (this is akin to group 1). Legit advertising agencies will, at either no cost or at slight cost,

do this for their clients (They make their profit from discounts allowed them by various ad media). Many will handle even the smallest account.

5. Sellers of "Imprints", co-published manuals, & catalogs (the "Chainletter Boys"). Here again, if the sales potential hadn't already been exhausted, they wouldn't advertise for competition.

6. Peddlers of servicing routes for dispensors or displays. They invariably demand a quite sizeable investment, from you, for the stock and machinery, and in return they guarantee to turn over established routes or contracts. Your margin is so low that you can't make a profit and when you want out you find yourself loaded down with goods that aren't returnable and promises that were never fulfilled.

7. The "Drop-Ship" merchants. You do the selling, keep your profit, send them their percentage and your own shipping label and they

in turn ship direct to your customer. While the product offered has usually been over-exposed and its' potential slim, in some cases, if the product is unique and useful, you can come out ahead of the game.

8. The "Agents" Wanted advertisers. While you must tread carefully, even here, you can proceed with some confidence if you are required to invest nothing but your time and effort (and if the product is in demand). Notable here are the major magazine distribution agencies or manufacturers or distributors of sensible and reputable products (steer clear of drugs, vitamins, health foods, salves, etc.).

In summation if; upon opening the reply to your initial inquiry, you find a request for money, throw it away! Some will even insist that you remit a CERTIFIED check, money, or curency (which they insist is perfectly safe—the post office department disagrees). They do this with the knowledge that once you see that you have been bilked, you will stop payment on a personal check. Remember; look before you leap, seek advice, and don't trust them if they won't trust you.

Ten Business Commandments

A thought provoking set of rules for success from the *Inspection News*.

1. Work Hard—Take the hardest job first every day.
2. Study Hard—The more you know, the easier and more effective is your work.
3. Have Initiative—Ruts often deepen into graves.
4. Love Your Work—There's a sense of satisfaction in doing your work well.
5. Be Exact—Accuracy is better than haste.
6. Have Courage—A stout heart will carry you through difficulties.
7. Be Friendly—Only friendly people become successful leaders.
8. Cultivate Personality—Personality is to the human what perfume is to the flower.
9. Wear A Smile—It opens the door into the sunshine beyond.
10. Do Your Best—For if you give to the world the best you have, the best will come back to you.

A Home Operated Accounting Business

David Tawwater had polio in 1950—two days before he was to leave for college football training. Formerly a righthander, he does everything left handed, having some functional use of his left hand and arm.

Dave said, "Before polio I had no training in accounting or bookkeeping. About the only thing I had in high school that directly helped me was typing, in fact I had planned to take engineering in college. In 1954, I finished a correspondence course in Higher Accounting, paid for by the Texas Rehabilitation Agency. I started doing some tax work and bookkeeping. A lot of my work came from people who had known me and who had been trying to do their own bookkeeping and tax work without knowing much about what they were doing. I put a sign out on the highway near my home and did a little advertising in our local newspaper.

"I didn't do too much those first two years. I wasn't able to work too hard and I had to learn a lot of things about small businesses and income tax as I went along. I found out there is a lot they don't teach you in a c c o u n t i n g courses—you have to learn it through experience. In 1955, I

netted about $700, but in 1957 netted over twice that amount. In 1958, my net income was just over $2300, and since then it has been increasing considerably every year.

"Most of my income is made during the first 3½ months of the year during income tax season. I have a great many people come back to me each year to prepare their own individual income tax returns.

"As for selling, there isn't much you can do in this type of business, except by reputation through your present clients. New business comes from people who have heard about my services from my present clients. This shows the importance of doing quality work and of being fair with people at all times."

"Other doctors should look into the idea of hiring the handicapped to relieve the typing burden on their office girls," say W. W. Glass, Jr., M.D. and Martin R. Haig, M.D. Joan Letulle, a C-6 level paraplegic, is their dictaphone typist.

How I Make Good Money Typing In My Home

by Joan Letulle

Independence is important! It is of the utmost importance to a handicapped person; he must find work which will help him to cease feeling like a burden to anyone. For those handicapped who must work at home, I have a few ideas —I hope you will find one which fits your abilities!

First, let me tell you of my own occupation which I chanced upon after trying many others. My tools of trade are a typewriter and a small medical dictionary—I am a dictaphone typist for an orthopedic surgeon. He provides the letterheads, carbons, second sheets, and the dictaphone transcriber. I type the letters here at home, then one of the office girls picks up the finished product! This has proven to be interesting work.

To explain further, I am a paraplegic with no leg movements whatsoever. How do I use the dictaphone? Simple! The foot pedal is on my desk; I push it down with my hand, listen to a sentence or two, then type. If any of you can type, just contact several doctors and offer your services. In fact, it's possible that other types of business offices could use this service, too.

Another outlet for someone with typing skill is typing for college students. Have someone from a nearby college put your name and phone number on their bulletin boards and you will get plenty of calls. Occasional newspaper ads are good advertising for this work. If you do good work, the students themselves will recommend you and you'll be kept busy. I know, for I did this myself for several years. Typing in the home can be expanded by letting your Chamber of Commerce know of your work and they will recommend you to out-of-towners who are in need of a public stenographer. Further ex-

Joan is paid the going rate of three dollars per belt. She types using her left hand and the eraser end of a pencil held in her right hand.

Unable to use her legs, Joan pushes down the dictaphone foot pedal with her hand, listens to a sentence or two, then types.

pansion of this could be a duplicating business. Yes, this takes a modest sum of money to start, but it can become quite lucrative with good advertising and by informing civic clubs and religious organizations of your service. Then, the key to success is extremely good service on bulletins, booklets, and letters.

A sideline occupation which I have had for years is being a Notary Public for our county. This is easy to maintain, takes little time, and has a small initial outlay —the price of a bond and a notary seal. When at home evenings, I'm available for this work and this helps people who cannot get it done in the daytime. Instructions and appointments of Notaries vary from state to state, but it would be easy to find out the requirements for your locality.

My next idea for handicapped self-employment is for those who may have been teacher or good student in school. Tutors are badly needed at all levels of education— elementary, high school, and college. Former teachers are, of course, best suited for this but a teaching certificate is not necessary. Let the faculty of a nearby school know you are available; tell them the grades and subjects you feel qualified to tutor. It's easier to work with one school as the teachers will give you a brief refresher course in your subject if needed, show you their method of teaching, and loan text books and answer books. Please don't hesitate to try this occupation; it's such rewarding work! Yes, I know about this too; I tutored for about four years!

Recently, I heard of a hobby which turned into a profitable business. Someone took a course in cake decorating and began taking orders in her home. Word spread of her fine work and soon she had

"Handicapped Texan For 1969" is the name of this citation from the Governor's Committee for Employment of the Handicapped being presented to Joan Letulle by Martin Dies, Secretary of State.

developed a business of renting everything needed for wedding or baby showers, from punch bowls to centerpieces! Initiative and creativity were the guiding forces in this enterprise.

My own two hobbies could someday turn into money-makers. I have taken two creative writing courses—one at Lamar State College of Technology in Beaumont, Texas, and a correspondence course from Famous Writers School. To date, I have sold four short stories and several articles to both handicapped and religious publications. A year ago I started taking oil painting lessons which I have thoroughly enjoyed. My paintings have been in three exhibits—including one in the State Capitol in Austin, Texas—and I have sold four paintings thus far. What is your hobby? Many times hobbies turn into big businesses!

For those of you who do not have the skills needed for these ideas, there are always the familiar standbys—greeting card selling, gift shops, magazine subscription selling, monitoring television commercials, telephone answering service, etc. Any business can grow; it's up to the person. All it takes is initiative, advertising, and a good selling job. We handicapped have to be good salesmen no matter what our occupation is; we must not only sell our wares but also ourselves and our abilities. That's why, for us, success is so much more satisfying.

So, good luck to you, and may independence soon be yours!

I Run A Transportation Service

Alex L. Maxwell, confined to a wheelchair since being injured in the Vietnam War in 1968 (T-4 and T-5) has found an answer to the transportation problems of disabled persons and at the same time has solved his own employment problem.

He started his own business,

Alex Maxwell, a paraplegic, provides transportation at ten cents less per mile than other local taxi services.

Handicapped Services, Inc., in Peoria, Illinois. It's a taxi service serving disabled persons and others who live within 50 miles of Peoria.

After returning home from the hospital, Maxwell decided to go into business for himself. So, he went to the local Service Corps of Retired Executives (SCORE) and the Small Business Administration for advice. He was advised to first gather facts necessary to establish a business like he had in mind.

Over a two year period he surveyed the potential market and studied such things as what licenses and insurance plans are needed and what the local taxi services charged. Then he took his savings, borrowed some more money and went into business.

There are many expenses a person starting such a business should know about before going too far. Maxwell was kind enough to list them for ACCENT. He payed $6,000 for a van with a raised top, $1,000 for a lift and $3,500 for 2-way radio equipment. Smaller expenses included: safety devices, insurance, a business telephone, advertising, a wheelchair, a portable ramp for use at inaccessible places, wages and uniforms for a driver, maintenance, an attorney, an accountant, office supplies, advertising and lettering for the van. His total gasoline bill for the first three months of this year is over $550.

He started the business last October and his business is continuing to grow rapidly. The van ser-

vice operates out of Maxwell's home from 9 a.m. to 5 p.m. seven days a week. He carries an average of 20 passengers a day and charges a little less than local taxis. Charges listed on his rate sheet range from $1.00 for the first mile to $45.50 for 50 miles.

The van, which is driven by his brother-in-law, can transport as many as seven passengers at a time; up to three in wheelchairs. Maxwell says that his brother-in-law's volunteer driving is helping to curb expenses in this early stage of his business.

"The van itself, complete with an electric lift, is one of my most effective forms of advertising," Maxwell says.

Transporting passengers for local agencies and institutions is a very important part of Maxwell's business. Two of his largest customers are the Illinois Public Aid Commission and the local United Cerebral Palsy chapter. He feels that it was important to secure agreements with as many agencies as possible in order to establish a solid core of steady income. One disadvantage he found in transporting persons for government agencies is the long time lag before he receives payment.

Nurses' Employment Service

by Russ Beeson

At the beginning of what I hoped would be a successful speed boat racing career in 1953 and at the age of twenty, I was admitted to the hospital with what was diagnosed as Bulbar Polio.

After nine months in the iron lung I gave birth to a rocking bed, which later was reduced to a chest respirator. In 1955 I was discharged from the hospital and moved back to my home in Walnut Creek, California.

After settling down for an extremely hot summer, I began to investigate the various possibilities of self-employment. A nurse friend of mine told me that a nurses' employment service was seriously needed in this area, so after some thinking and planning and with the cooperation of my vocational rehabilitation counselor I obtained my license

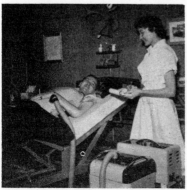

from the Labor Commissioner of California in October of 1956 and the RuBee Nurses Registry was open for business.

Not only was this successful in itself, but it set off a chain of events that never ceases to amaze me. While working out the problem of a telephone that I could operate with my head, I met a salesman for the telephone company who was a member of the local Jaycees. Later I was initiated and made an honorary member in good standing with full privileges. I was kept very busy conducting telephone campaigns and was honored in July, 1957, as a recipient of the "Jaycee of the Month" award. From my personal experience I would highly recommend that anyone in our position investigate the possibility of becoming active in a civic group or service organization.

I have a specially constructed bed mounted on retractable wheels which fits into the rear of our station wagon which makes it easy for me to travel to various association meetings, friends homes, boat races, outdoor movies, etc.

Although I have made no earth-shattering achievements, I believe that these past experiences and my plans for the future have brought me closer to my goal of living a normal life.

by Marie D. Benford

Eric Mohn is president of Rehab Transportation. He feels other handicapped people could have their own businesses by starting similar services.

*Operating his business from his home,
quadriplegic Eric Mohn provides*

Special Transportation For The Disabled In The Nation's Capital

"America is the land of the mobile," says Eric Mohn, a young quadriplegic, "a fact known to hundreds of thousands of handicapped persons across the nation who have places to go but no way to get there."

There are more than 150,000 disabled persons in Washington, D. C. and in the nearby Maryland suburbs —60% of whom cannot use taxis or buses.

Eric Mohn well knows the feeling of being "trapped." Unable to depend on either taxi cabs or buses, he would sit while undergoing therapy at the Rusk Rehabilitation Institute in New York waiting for his parents who might, when they visited, take him in their car if weather permitted.

"It got very depressing," he says. Especially for a young man who had, up until eight years ago when his neck was broken in an automobile accident, led a very active life.

Last September Eric enrolled in a program at George Washington University's Medical Center that has proven to be the turning point in his life. The program, headed by Thomas Shworles, was involved in finding "home type" employment for the handicapped.

It was Shworles who first, indirectly, gave Eric the idea for providing a service of low-cost transportation. About two-thirds of Shworles' clients were unable to attend meetings because they could either not afford the transportation available—or simply could not find transportation.

He approached Eric for the use of Eric's private vehicle—a Volkswagon bus with a handi-ramp. The idea of Rehab Transportation took hold in Eric's mind. He got busy on the phone calling hospitals, clinics, societies and schools. "Yes," came the response, "we have a need for this type of service. If you can provide it, we'll use it."

This 7-seat bus with ramp for wheelchairs provides safe, comfortable rides and enables handicapped customers to go where and when they want to go.

That same month, Eric and two other quadriplegics whom he had met at George Washington, 23-year old Surinder Dhillon of the Washington District and 21-year-old John Collins of Alexandria pooled almost $1,000 each to buy a seven-seat bus with ramps for wheelchairs and formed Rehab Transportation.

Eric heads the business. Since one of his partners is still in college and the other has found employment as a computer agent for COMSAT, they depend on Eric to handle the operation from his Rockville home.

Rehab provides personalized, round-trip transportation for disabled people at low costs. Presently, the service charges $4.50 to $8 for round-trip ambulatory persons and $10 to $14 round-trip for individuals in wheel chairs.

"We hope," Eric said "to reduce these costs as our business grows." Up until three weeks ago Rehab Transportation was growing very slowly. The fledgling company was struggling because, as Eric explained, "We started out doing everything wrong. Our timing was poor. The economy was hurting. It was the wrong time of the year and our capital was limited.

"Our first bit of business was transporting handicapped children and our consciences wouldn't allow us to charge more than the barest minimum. We did this for the first two months—all the while trying to attract new customers. Just driving down the streets in the bus—in my wheelchair—brought us a few customers. But not until the Information Center for Handicapped Children in Washington donated a small bus for us to use, followed by a small loan did our business perk up."

Now six months old Rehab Transportation, Inc. has three vehicles, two full-time drivers and is considering taking on another part-time for weekends and evenings.

"We have more business than we can handle. We've acquired a lawyer and look to him for good business direction and also we've had some publicity from local newspapers."

Recently, Rehab was employed by the President's Committee on Employment of the Handicapped to transport Richard and Robert Santin, twin brothers, aged 32, lifelong muscular dystrophy victims, who had been called from Nebraska to Washington to receive a national award.

Eric starts his day at about 9:00AM on the phone. He uses an intercom telephone system that's kept busy well into the evening. "It's taken us six months to get where we are now—showing a profit. But, we do have bills that we incurred earlier that we haven't met as yet—so we'll either have to put more of our money into the Corporation or issue stock. Our lawyer has advised that we issue stock—private issue to a select number of buyers."

How Rehab Transportation meets this small problem isn't of great concern to either Mohn or his partners. Instead they are thrilled with the problem of having their phone busy ringing. They promise their customers safe, comfortable rides—at low costs. The handicapped, he says, no longer will be forced to ask their friends or family to tag along. Their drivers are non-handicapped. But what's of greatest importance, and satisfaction is that Rehab is opening doors. If and when you want to, you can catch Sammy Davis at the Shoreham or you can spend the day at the Smithsonian—the choice is up to you. Just call Rehab.

Gift Fruit Business

Tommy Robertson went into his own Texas gift fruit business after he had polio in 1951. Tommy handles most of his own correspondence and types his mailing lists (numbering in the hundreds) by using a stylus in his mouth. He sells fancy gift fruit, ruby red and white grapefruit and Texas golden oranges.

homebound computer programmer earns

$160⁰⁰ A WEEK!

Can a person paralyzed from the neck down earn $160 a week at home? Many people doubt it. However, good income and respectable jobs can be possible for many severely disabled.

Douglas T. Boyce, a computer programmer for the Lynchburg, Va. office of General Electric, will vouch for that.

In 1969 Boyce competed in the Virginia high school wrestling quarterfinal in which he suffered a back injury at the C 5-6 level

which left him paralyzed, with the exception of wrist movement in his hands.

Boyce finished high school while recuperating at the University of Virginia Hospital. Later, he went to Woodrow Wilson Rehabilitation Center (WWRC).

While there he became a candidate for a pilot project in computer programming. His rehabilation counselor, John Lucado, initiated talks with General Electric about employment there for Boyce after completion of the program. One aspect which sets this program apart from others is that a job committment is necessary before enrollment.

The eight to twelve month computer programming course at WWRC was established through the cooperative efforts of IBM and WWRC to train severely disabled persons like Boyce as computer programmers and computer terminal operators.

It is financed by the Virginia Department of Vocational Rehabilitation and the Federal Rehabilitation Services Administration.

The GE division for which Boyce works as the first graduate of this pilot project uses a Honeywell 6000 series equipped for remote processing. By using a TermiNet 300 equipped with an acoustic coupler and cassette tape, Boyce can "talk" to the main computer system in the GE office.

Boyce works a regular 8-hour day in a room in his home which was remodeled and rewired to handle the equipment and the additional electric load.

Work assignments are either hand-carried to him or given verbally over the telephone. He then completes the logic design, writes the COBOL code and enters it into the cassette tape to be transmitted by the TermiNet terminal to the computer site.

The special training project promises to be a successful one. Anyone interested can get more information by writing to the Director, Woodrow Wilson Rehabilitation Center, Fishersville, Va. 22939.

Dance, Concert Promotion

BY JUNE PRICE

Bill Troute with Sonny and Cher, one of the well-known groups he has booked as president of Monarch Productions. Others include Chicago, The Blues Image, Three Dog Night, and Friends of Distinction.

As a quadriplegic with very little movement, Bill Troute climbed the steps and reached the top. In this article, he tells how it happened and gives some of his ideas that could work for you, too!

Whatever the extent of your beliefs in it, all will at least admit astrology is "interesting." The accuracy of horoscopes is frequently disputed, though it is also sometimes astonishingly true.

Sagittarians, for example, are said to be "vigorous and energetic; enjoy activity, outdoor sports and games; have a strong interest in education, philosophy, and the arts; they have intuitive minds and high aspirations." As for an occupation, "choose a career involving distribution, such as television, radio, journalism (etc.)." It's said you are to "avoid anything small or limited in scope." And, "many are the far places you can travel: actually, mentally, and spiritually."

All Sagittarians may not fit this partial blueprint, but as far as William D. Troute is concerned, the sign reflects him to the letter.

Bill may have had his astrological sign in his favor, but he had little else going for him when polio made him a quadriplegic at 17 when he was a senior in high school.

Now at 32, Bill Troute is president of Monarch Productions, a dance-concert promotion company, and deals almost exclusively in the youth market.

How Bill climbed the "long and winding road" to success is encouraging.

Bill went through a quite typical period of depression and self-pity after polio hit. For the next five years, he "watched T.V., talked on the phone, read, wrote, painted, brooded, swore, drank a lot, and did wretched phone sales."

Then it happened. "The car club I belonged to decided to throw a dance and only I and a couple of other guys were willing to work on it. I had played in my own band in high school before polio hit and so I elected to contact the groups.

Bill continued: "When I heard and watched these groups rehearse, I was really star struck. This provided me with a lot of ego gratification and a feeling of self-importance. Other benefits I derived included, most importantly, one of

the leader's encouragement for me to try to book his and other groups. He patiently explained the procedures, and upon my first attempt to book the act I succeeded and made $70 commission! I thought this was so fantastic — all this money, and glory. What an ego trip!"

Bill decided to work with the idea of promoting more bands for future dances. The work could be done from his home, his only major problem being the telephone.

After a little investigation, he found the telephone company had a phone he could use, after a little modification. It consisted of a little square metal box with two upright "L"-shaped levers (one is a hold key; the other selects one of his two lines).

"When I push the appropriate lever," Bill explains, " a light comes on, the operator asks what number I want, and places the call." Bill wears a head set. "The phone also has holes on the back so that it may be hung on the wall next to my bed so that I can use it lying down, and it also fits in a box on my lap board for use when sitting," he explains.

Bill admits his business got much rougher than his first encounter with getting a band for his car club dance led him to believe.

"Some goals normally realized are thwarted by physical obstacles such as general inability to rush from place to place (for last minute appointments, for example), the necessity for rapid and fairly constant note taking, and minor prejudices. There is considerable telephone work, correspondence and a high overhead," he says.

Although he does much of the work himself, Bill maintains that an office girl doing the general clerical work, and at least one able-bodied assistant are a physical necessity.

The job of president of a dance-concert promotion company is no easy task. It involves booking bands of varying degrees of fame for "anyone who has the money to hire them;" half-planning and promoting shows; some record promoting; and designing brochures. Being a free-agent he is able to book anyone and everyone who is currently popular, plus unknown variety and specialty acts or bands.

Bill has handled such groups as Sonny & Cher, Chicago, The Blues Image, Three Dog Night, Poco, Flying Burrto Bros., Spirit, Steve Miller, Linda Ronstadt, Friends of Distinction, and many, many others.

As if his job weren't enough to keep him busy, he also attends a nearby junior college nights studying liberal arts and sociology.

Starting his business from his home, he was able to financially establish himself well enough to soon afford a car (now a '69 Grand Prix), a hired driver, and an office away from home.

Bill's insights into success and failure for the handicapped person may lead many up that long and winding road.

He stated, as most handicapped people have found, that transportation is the largest single factor holding a handicapped person back from acquiring more freedom. Prejudices come second, along with obvious physical limitations (both individual and environmental).

Advice to other handicapped people? I asked him these questions:

Q. What do you consider to be the one most important thing needed to overcome a handicap?

A. Confidence. An ability to ignore your obvious limitations.

Q. Do you feel a handicapped person should try for seemingly unobtainable goals?

A. Yes, if they are only seemingly unobtainable. No, otherwise. If a goal is unobtainable, then frustration is inevitable. Re-evaluate.

Q. What advice would you give to someone who feels his world has limited horizons?

A. Expand them. Read (wide variety of topics, political, social, ecological, philosophical. etc.); do anything within one's power to change society for the better (eliminate racialism; stop the rape of the environment; promote birth control; eliminate poverty through promoting guaranteed income, health care for all, etc.); love your brother; talk to as wide a variety of persons as possible in order to better understand them and yourself; try to remove from office politicians not in tune with, or in opposition to, these issues.

Of all that Bill said, one thing hit it all right on the nose: "Be realistic and optimistic." About Sagittarians, astrologers say, "Your optimism never waivers." And Bill Troute is a Sagittarian!

Accounting
by C. A. Lufburrow

Early one morning in the spring of 1957, Bob awoke unable to move his left leg. Alarmed and helpless, he called his wife. Mary lost no time. With a brief prayer to God for help, she left her two-year old daughter with the folks and started driving him to the nearest hospital, 37 miles away.

Polio hit hard. They put him in an iron lung. His whole body was paralyzed, except his right toes and fingers. Bob must have constant care. Nurses were scarce. Mary was a schoolteacher, but she volunteered anyway, and was given a two weeks intensive course.

At home and at church, folks

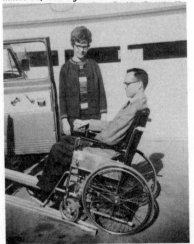

One happy couple! The result of determination, courage and a lot of work.

were praying. Mary wrote to other more distant friends. As a result Bob later reported an inner peace they had never known before. (Phil. 4:7.)

For the next 14 months he was in the hospital. The first six weeks Mary worked the 3 to 11 P.M. shift, caring for him. After that she was with him as much as possible, for during his hospital time their second child, a boy, was born. "Truly," reflected Bob, "God has given me a wonderful family."

When they told him he might go home, Mary had to find a new home, and move, nearer medical attention. Along with Bob came his rocking bed, wheelchair, respirator and hoist. But with three waiting for him, it was a marvelous homecoming!

At first he could be up only 2 hours a day. He had some use of his arms and hands, but had difficulty in breathing. For another year he had daily therapy.

Born and brought up on a midwestern farm, Bob loved farming. Their dream had always been a new farm home. Except for about two years army service, which took him to Korea, farming was their life.

He reconsidered the future and made a difficult decision, to study accounting by correspondence. To hold a pencil he went back to the hospital for a muscle transplant.

More work than he can take care of! Bob does bookkeeping, tax work and sells insurance—all from this office located in the basement of his new home.

That took several weeks for a satisfactory adjustment. After two years he received a Certificate in Accounting. Through advertising, work gradually came in.

In 1959, Bob drew his first house plans. Their new home, in town, has an office in the basement and an elevator. Actual building, with Mary overseeing the work, was finished just before Christmas. How they thanked God that Christmas Day!

By the fall of 1960, Bob could spend half of each day in his office. In addition to the accounting work, he sold auto insurance and drew two house plans for others, while taking care of his three year old son. Mary took their little girl to kindergarten, and taught school half a day. In the afternoon she did her housework while the other three rested. In 1961 both were attending night classes. Bob was learning to prepare income tax returns, and Mary was working toward her degree.

Bob loves his Lord and wants to serve Him. When their little church outgrew the building, they asked Bob to draw the plans for a new one. Now he is on the Church Board and very active.

Each summer the family takes a two weeks camping trip. Their car has double side doors so he can run his electric wheelchair in. The car is equipped with a bed, a patient lift on top, respirator and a tent which attaches to the side, for the children. They all love the outdoors and have great times together.

Bob lives a happy, normal life. His tax work, bookkeeping and insurance now keep him busy full time, an eight hour day, with extra help needed for tax seasons. Mary now has her degree. In addition to teaching, housekeeping and family care, she finds time to act as secretary and chauffeur for Bob.

Bob and Mary appreciate their blessings. His advice is: This troubled world has only a few passing days compared to eternity with Christ. Proverbs 3: 5 and 6 are favorite verses of mine: "Trust in the Lord with all thine heart, and lean not to thine own understanding. In all thy ways acknowledge Him, and He shall direct thy paths."

Baby Sitters Registry

Jean Denecke operates the Rock-A-Bye Sitters Registry which is licensed and bonded by the state of Michigan. Jean also had polio 11 1/2 years ago, is what could be called a severely handicapped person, and can only sit up from 4 1/2 to 5 hours a day in her wheelchair. The rest of her time is spent in bed, but business goes on as usual.

The number of qualified baby sitters in her active file totals nearly 60. Each one has been interviewed personally by Jean and she has carefully checked the references of each. All of the sitters are adults.

Are you interested in starting a baby sitter Registry? Jean's first advice is, "First of all you must inquire about a state license. Mine

Jean Denecke, keeps nearly 60 baby sitters busy. With her, shown left, is her housekeeper Della Pelmore. This story is more proof that nothing is really impossible.

is $50, plus a $10 surety bond per year. No city license is required here." She goes on to say, "I will explain my method of operation. I register customers for the year at $12.50 for the year's service (a year from the day they register, not the calendar year). A registered customer pays a baby sitter 60c per hour with a four hour minimum, plus 50c for transportation. If the customer is not registered, the charge is 85c per hour with the four hour minimum and 50c for transportation. 25c per hour comes to the Registry, which is collected by the sitter and she, in turn, reimburses me. We also do maternity and vacation calls for our customers. The rate is $8 per day for two childern or less, $9 per day for more than two children. It is $1 per day more in each case for an unregistered customer. 10% of this money goes to the Registry."

She has limited her business numerically and geographically so she can handle it herself with the assistance of her housekeeper and a rented telephone answering recorder from the telephone company. She uses a simple card index file marking a registered customer with a star. Each call is written on the customer's card with the name of the sitter who filled the call. Statements are mailed once a month.

Jean said, "I find the telephone answering recorder to be of invaluable assistance and much less expensive and confusing than having someone in to help do this." The recorder is on all the time and when the calling customer tells the date and time a baby sitter is wanted, this is recorded. Later then, her housekeeper takes the calls off the recorder and relays them to Jean to write down in her date book.

This business started small with just two sitters, one of whom was a friend. She advertised for sitters,

always interviewing them personally, and checking all references herself. When the local newspapers heard of her new business, they wrote feature stories with photographs, and Jean attributes much of her success to this publicity.

Jean enthusiastically says, "I've made many real friends, and have been of genuine help by offering a much needed service and of course it has given me occupational therapy beyond the 'something to do' stage."

Bookkeeping At Home

A-1 bookkeeping, tax returns and notary public appear impressively at the top of Larry Cunningham's own letterhead stationery. Larry, who broke his neck in a diving accident in 1953, is a quadraplegic with some use of his arms and only a little use of his hands. The California State Department of Vocational Rehabilitation provided the money for a correspondence course in bookkeeping and income tax work, an electric duplicating machine, an adding machine and a file cabinet. In July of 1956 he started in business.

Larry said, "Having limited use of my hands I do most of the bookkeeping on an electric typewriter,

but write information while interviewing tax customers. I intend to specialize in income tax because it has good possibilities. By having three small bookkeeping accounts

Larry Cunningham and his wife Aggie earned $2,069 last year, and are well on the way toward being successful.

and doing income tax my average monthly profits for 1959 was almost $200. My income from filling out tax returns doubled the past year and should continue to increase in the coming years.

"Upon the advice of a tax accountant friend, I became a notary public. It is necessary to have a business license here and helpful to have a business phone. It is essential to have tax guides and current reports to keep up to date with changing tax rules and regulations.

"To acquire customers, advertising in the phone book is very helpful, but better yet is a satisfied customer referring someone else. My business hours are from nine a.m. to eight p.m., seven days a week which is an added convenience for people unable to come during the day because of their employment."

While Larry's income is building up, his wife, Aggie, has a full time job. They employ a baby sitter to care for their six year old daughter. She also helps Larry during the day.

To show progress made his net profit for the year 1957 was just $759. In 1958 he cleared $1,288 and in 1959 this jumped to $2,069.

Well on the way toward making a big success of his business he gives special thanks to his good wife, Aggie, and his parents for their encouragement and faith in him.

His advice to someone interested in a similar business, "The more you study, the better. Start small and grow as you learn. Don't take on more work than you can handle and take a personal interest in each customer's problems."

Computer Technologist

Severe rheumatoid arthritis doesn't keep Surinder Dhillon from running his own business, Rehab Computer, Inc. He is a computer technologist and works from his own home with several employees.

Telephone Answering Service

by Cornelia M. Parkinson

Something special in telephone service is available in Marion, Ohio. Mrs. Frieda Moore, owner-operator of Apt Answering Service, has twenty-three phones on the desk in the sunny office of her home. Each phone has a distinctive ring and must be kept in a particular spot to enable Mrs. Moore, who is totally blind, to identify it.

Among her clients are companies which handle lumber, snack foods, real estate, music, construction, office machines, and utilities. Most of the phones are answered only during regular office hours; a few are on 16-hour and 24-hour call. Except for occasional substitute help, Mrs. Moore handles her tricky job alone with charm, cheerfulness, and unflappable calm. Her remarkable mental filing system holds hundreds of pieces of information pertaining to the operation of each company, the whereabouts of their service men, and any phone numbers she is likely to have to call in Marion or elsewhere.

She does not depend on memory for message taking. For this she uses three devices: a flexible holder devised by her brother to hold the telephone handset; her Braille watch; and her Braille writing plate. Each call is recorded on the daysheets for that company, and becomes a part of her business records.

In dialing the phone, she uses a touch system with her index finger in the 3 position (from which she reaches 4 and 5) middle finger at 2, ring finger at 1; or with her index finger at 8 (reaching to 7 and 6) and the other fingers on 9 and 0.

Slim, attractive Mrs. Moore started in business in February, 1963, with two telephones. When the Marion-Morrow-Delaware County oil boom began, she would sometimes have four new phones installed in a day's time. Though "not ready yet" for a Braille switchboard, she feels that, with a bigger desk, she could handle a few more clients.

Mrs. Moore, who lost her sight at age eleven, has a very realistic, constructive view of her handicap. "I wouldn't want to encourage anyone who became blind just to get a box of tissues and cry it up," she says. "There are so many opportunities nowadays for blind people if they'll just take advantage of them. I know I'd never be satisfied just to sit and draw a government check when I'm perfectly able to support myself and my daughter Rita."

In her rare free time, energetic Frieda enjoys doing all her own housework—ironing, cooking, waxing floors, and washing windows. She keeps her cheerful six-room home immaculate, welcomes a steady stream of weekend visitors. She likes to read the stories and articles in Braille-printed magazines. With a substitute minding the phones, she can sometimes spend an hour or two shopping with her sister, or roaming the woods on her brother's farm.

Of her business she says, "I really enjoy this—it gives you a constant education. You learn so much about so many different things, and you meet so many nice people who make you feel your work is really worthwhile. I guess a person could hardly ask more than that."

Another Telephone Answering Service

How the Straubs, both in wheelchairs and on welfare, got a loan to buy a business they could operate in their home.

by Mary and Leonard Kennedy

The ringing of telephones twenty-fours a day may be an annoyance to some, but it's music to the ears of Dorothy and Richard Straub. And with ninety-eight clients on their answering service, they hear plenty of this telephone music.

"Actually," explains Dottie, "it all came about rather by accident. We had spent nearly ten years being grateful for our monthly welfare check. But you get to a point in life when you must do something to change."

Because of Richard's illness, which has kept him in a wheelchair for seventeen years and has recently been complicated by a heart attack, Dorothy called the family doctor often. Many of these calls went through an answering service, and Dottie became acquainted by phone with the owner of the business. One day in a conversation the lady told Dorothy she was thinking of selling the service.

"I didn't give the news much thought at first," recalls Dottie. "But after I thought about it for a few days, I got curious and called to see what she wanted for the business. It seemed to me that it might be a good business for me to run from my wheelchair."

Dorothy struggled for a year to borrow money from local banks to buy the answering service but all she got for her efforts was a handful of papers. And to top this off

Richard takes a handful of the day's records.

another party was about to buy the business.

"I hit rock bottom," Dorothy says.

She had almost decided the best thing to do was let her plans go with the wind when Richard's rehabilitation representative asked Dottie about the prospects for getting the answering service. She poured out her problems.

"He could see I was discouraged," she says. "But he told me

Dorothy makes a record of each client's call.

to try again. He would help me this time."

Dorothy wasn't so sure anybody could help. But she called the owner to find out if she would take a chance on her again. "We've got some help behind us this time," Dottie told her.

The owner still considered Dorothy as a prospective buyer. In the meantime the rehabilitation representative contacted SCORE, a re-

tired businessmen's association that helps small businesses to get started.

SCORE's representative approved of the business and got more information from banks to help Dottie and Dick qualify for a $5,000 loan through the Small Business Administration.

After two years of struggling, the business deal went through. And in April 1970, Dottie and Richard took over.

Dorothy worked with the former owner for several weeks to learn the business and in that time had a small addition built onto their home for the switchboard.

The Straubs are pleased with their success. They have added fifty new clients to the forty-eight they purchased and they employ a full-time switchboard operator and two relief girls as well as a bookkeeper.

Richard's happy that Dottie got curious about the service. "We don't live high," he says, "but we're on our own."

To Dorothy, who has cerebral palsy, running their own business is reward enough. But in 1971 California's State Department of Rehabilitation honored her with the "Rehabilitant of the Year" award.

Dottie and Richard enjoy sharing their success. They support themselves and two of their four children who are still at home. And what's more they can share with Uncle Sam. As Dottie tells it: "This may sound silly, but when I wrote out the check for taxes for the first time in nine years, I cried!"

Private Security Police And Sales

Roger Liephart, paralyzed from the neck down, travels 2,500 miles a month supervising his two businesses

by Dick Vader

In his security car, Roger talks by mobile phone to one of his men.

Roger shows the Amway merchandise displayed in his home.

On March 3, 1960, nine weeks before he was to graduate from Parma Senior High School in Cleveland, Ohio, Roger Liephart suffered a broken neck doing a forward flip on the gym trampoline.

The doctor told his parents that if he lived, he would be paralyzed for the rest of his life, but warned he could die from complications in five or six years.

Even though Roger is paralyzed, he has accomplished more in the past 13 years than many physically-able men do in a lifetime.

After three months in intensive care and seven months in a long-term care hospital, Roger and his family were in debt due to medical bills not covered by insurance. Although he received hundreds of cards, letters and donations, and several benefits for him were held, there still wasn't enough money to pay all the bills.

But Roger, who had been a crew manager in a magazine business in high school, resumed his business from his bed and wheelchair in 1961. He also was introduced to Amway — a home-care product business — and, in less than two years, was able to pay off more than $5,000 in medical bills.

His Amway business became so profitable he gradually gave up his magazine enterprise. His bedroom is his office. Ohio Bell engineered a special telephone for him that he could use as he regained some movement of his arms, although he was not able to use his fingers. He learned to type with a pencil inserted through a special device on his left hand, and a Royal typewriter was donated to him.

Roger had always been interested in law enforcement work, and in 1962, he organized a volunteer group called the Parma Radio Patrol. His men traveled in cars, assisting the regular police in looking for stolen cars, helping at accidents, etc. The Parma Radio Patrol was changed to the Cuyahoga County Highway Safety Patrol in 1966. In the fall of 1969, Roger and a friend, Ralph Watkins, organized Topp Security as

assistant on Amway deliveries to customers, and on Wednesday evening, attends an Amway business meeting. On Friday and Saturday evenings, Roger is on the road, supervising his men in an unmarked car. Roger travels 2,500 miles a month, with both his Amway and police businesses combined. He puts in about 25-30 hours a week with his Amway business and 30 hours with his police business. Topp Security has three fully-equipped cars which patrol part of the West Side of Cleveland. They pay special attention to their private accounts and also assist Cleveland police.

In 13 years, Roger has done quite a bit — first, a magazine business with 2,200 accounts, then

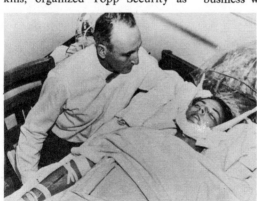

Things looked bad after the accident. In April 1960 Roger lay in intensive care with his father sitting over him. (Cleveland Press photo)

a private police agency.

Roger is a very busy man. His day begins at 10 a.m. when he opens his morning mail and starts receiving and putting through calls relating to both his Amway and police businesses. Tuesdays and Thursdays, Roger accompanies his

an Amway business with 500 retail accounts and 20 commercial accounts, a volunteer police organization, and now a regular police agency. He has an active social life, goes on dates, and is truly enjoying living.

Radio And Television Monitoring And Telephone Surveys

By Margaret Kuehlthau

In Tucson, Arizona, a young arthritic who can move only his jaw, his eyes and his right hand ever so slightly has built up a business which he conducts from his bed, using an ingenious telephone setup.

Adrian Van de Verde Jr., age 30, speaks of his room as "Utopia—300 square feet of it." "My room is much more interesting than I am," he says jokingly. Interesting as the room may be, it is no more remarkable than the young man whose indomitable spirit is reflected in every corner. His body may be bedbound (he calls himself a "mattress-naut" as opposed to an astronaut), but his mind soars and his conversation sparkles with positive thinking and forward-looking plans.

From his prone, almost immobile

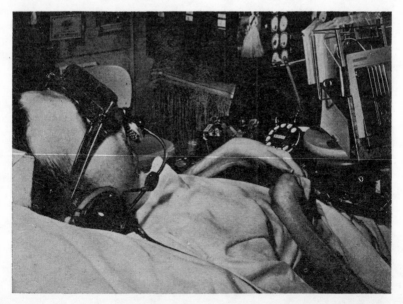

position, he conducts his share of a business in which he is a partner with a mobile arthritic, Frank Swartz. Together they operate the Southwest Communications Control. The address is Van de Verde's room, which he describes as "a coffee house, living quarters, and filter center for our business."

But to get back to the beginning of his handicap . . . Afflicted with arthritis and confined to his bed almost constantly since the age of 10, Van de Verde determined to keep busy.

It has not been easy. At the age of 21, with the aid of special teachers, he graduated from high school. He tried hobby after hobby only to know frustration. He wanted a job that would be profitable. Today, to this capable young man, shaving is a nuisance and a "waste of time." He has too many other interesting things to do.

Fated to remain bedfast because his joints are so extensively fused, no one could know better than he the need for a handicapped person to feel useful and wanted, so he made plans to develop a business in which he could hire other "unemployables." With his partner, he organized a company to handle radio and TV monitoring and tele-phone surveys. It puts to use the special talents available among arthritics and other handicapped and it eases the endless hours of boredom endured by the bedridden.

To get into operation, Van de Verde had to have means of contact with the clients on the outside. He did not have strength enough to press buttons nor could he lift a telephone receiver to his ear. The partners refused to accept defeat and an installer-repairman for the Mountain States Telephone and Telegraph Company came to their rescue. By improvising and adding levers to standard telephone equipment, a "hold" box for answering calls was put into operation. It can be operated with little more than a butterfly touch. With a telephone operator's headphone and a receiver placed on his head by his parents, Van de Verde is all set for business. In his right hand he grasps a light weight plastic stick. Like a magic wand, it opens the door to every facet of his existence.

With his "wand," Van de Verde presses levers which open the outside door leading into his room, raise and lower his bed, swing the turntable before him on which is placed his reading material, control his phonograph, radio and TV set,

MASTER OF ALL HE SURVEYS. Adrian Van de Verde Jr., 30, bedfast arthritic, is a partner in Southwest Communications Control. Prisms attached to his glasses expand his vision to the right and left. With the aid of a telephone operator's headgear and specially constructed equipment, he is able to conduct his share of business from his bed.

and most important of all—make it possible for him to dial outside numbers and to answer his telephone.

Ingenious devices, all of them, and according to Van de Verde, inexpensive enough to be within the financial reach of any homebound handicapped person.

No job is too small for their business to accept, and Van de Verde wishes that merchants and organizations needing surveys would realize this fact. "We have great talent among the handicapped." he believes. "The people who do our ratings and surveys do it on a scale applicable to the national scene. The quality of our work is high."

"Even $5 a month, earned independently by a handicapped person, gives a tremendous psychological boost. The most heart-breaking part of my work comes when I must inform other handicapped persons that there is not enough work to keep them all busy."

Pointing to himself as an example, he maintains that there is no phase of limitation in which a person cannot be productive to some extent. "I believe that one is first of all a human being who needs to feel useful and productive. Give a handicapped person a job—no matter 'how small—and say, 'Do the best you can.' "To exist, a guy has got to have hope."

Telephone Reminder Service
by Joyce Nelms

If you have a telephone (preferably one with a single line), a pleasant speaking voice, and enjoy talking to people, then you have all of the assets necessary to start a telephone reminder service. You can be your own boss and adjust your working hours to your liking.

There are many groups of professional men in every city and town; The Medical Society, Business Men's Associations, Chamber of Commerce, Professional Engineers and Architects, just to name a few. Most of them have monthly dinner meetings. The officer in charge of reservations must know how many members to expect for dinner so

he can inform the restaurant or hotel which supplies the food. Otherwise, it would be a little like the bride who prepared an intimate dinner for two, only to discover at the last minute that her husband had invited a dozen of the "boys" home for chow.

A letter is usually mailed to each member by the organization, telling them the date, time and place of the meeting and in most cases a self-addressed card is enclosed which the member is asked to fill out and return. However, Mr. Member is often so engrossed in personal and business affairs that he doesn't take time to fill out the card, or it is pushed under a stack of letters and forgotten.

This is where a telephone reminder service can be more efficient. A phone call to Mr. Member will take only a few minutes and the added personal touch will often increase attendance. And, with postage rates ever-increasing, the group will discover it actually costs less than the old post card method.

You can try any one of two methods to offer your telephone services. One, by letters or personal phone calls to the presidents or chairmen of the professional groups. They may be listed in your telephone directory or may be available by calling your local newspaper or Chamber of Commerce. Two, by placing an eye-catching ad in the newspaper. It might read something like this: "Let my reminder service help you to increase the efficiency of and attendance at your dinner-meetings. For information, call . . . . "

Many groups have one hundred or more members, and after you have accustomed yourself to the work, you may be able to make up to 500 calls in an eight hour day. This will give you an idea of how many accounts you will be able to handle.

To keep your records straight, try the following: Buy a small loose-leaf notebook, paste a strip of tape across the book, and write the name of the organization whose members will be listed therein, e.g., The Medical Society. Now, have a separate page for each member's name, writing the last name first. Beneath that, list both his

Joyce Nelms enjoys talking to people and makes money by doing so.

home and business number. Next, write the names of the months of the year in which the group will hold meetings. Then, as you make your calls, you can make notations.

Now you are ready to begin your calls. Always be brief, but courteous. You might say something like this:

"Hello Mr. Member, (smile and your voice will sound cheerful) my name is Joyce Nelms and I'm calling to remind you of the Chamber of Commerce meeting Tuesday, August 14th. Are you planning to attend?" Or, you might change the last sentence to, "Do you wish to make a dinner reservation?"

If Mr. Member explains that he has other commitments for that evening, then simply say, "Thank you. We hope you will be able to come next month," and hang up. It can be helpful if you try to arouse interest in a meeting by mentioning something about the program, such as the guest speaker and his topic.

You may call at Mr. Member's office during the daytime hours, or his home in the evening. After telephoning him a number of times, you will learn certain things about his schedule or himself that will help you save time in the future. If you call Mr. Member and his wife tells you he bowls on Monday evenings, make a note of this in your book, just above his name, and this will save you the wasted effort of calling on an evening when he is not at home.

Also, if Mrs. Member should tell you that although her husband still maintains his membership but he is inactive because of an illness, or a permanent conflict of meeting nights, make a note of this so you won't telephone again.

There are "Do's and Don'ts" in common telephone courtesy and these are especially important if telephoning is your profession. Here are a few to keep in mind as you work.

DON'T talk with chewing gum, cough drops, or candy in your mouth. The only movable object in your mouth while talking should be your tongue.

DON'T cough or clear your throat into the mouthpiece. If you have a frog in your throat, or feel the urge to cough, try to attend to such matters before getting your party on the line. But if a cough or

sneeze should escape you, remember to say "excuse me please."

DON'T shout at Mr. Member if you discover he is hard of hearing and asks you to repeat the message. Just raise the tone of your voice slightly, and speak more slowly.

DON'T lose patience with Mr. Member even though he may be cross and bite your head off once in a while. Everyone has personal problems, and you may have interrupted his after dinner nap, or favorite TV show. Keep a pleasant tone in your voice and be even more cheerful than usual. Chances are he'll greet you more pleasantly the next time.

DON'T have a TV set blaring next to you, or any other noises such as striking clocks, chattering children, etc.

DO speak slowly and distinctly into the mouthpiece. Decide exactly what you are going to say before you make the call, and try to convey the message without any "Uhs" or stammering. Remember the old adage about "haste makes waste." If you speak too rapidly, you may have to repeat your message.

DO try to learn the correct pronunciation of difficult-to-pronounce names. The first time you call, if you are in doubt, ask for the correct pronunciation, then make a note of it above the name in your notebook. This will guide you in the future.

DO have all of the information concerning the meeting before you when you call. Remember YOU are the voice of the group you are calling for. If he asks a question you can't answer, put him in contact with someone who can answer it or tell him you will find out and call him back right away.

Remember, good news travels fast, and if Mr. Member is favorably impressed with your courtesy, he will be likely to recommend your telephone service to other groups.

As time goes by, you will find short cuts which will simplify your work. You will get co-operation from the group itself. If they send out a monthly newsletter, ask them to print a paragraph about your telephone service.

When the calls have been completed, turn the figures over to the Program Chairman.

Now comes the BEST part . . . what to charge for your telephone service. After you get going, you will find you can make as many as sixty calls in an hour. If you charge five cents for each person contacted, you can average two dollars per hour.

Turn on your telephone charm and you'll find that operating a telephone reminder service is both pleasant and profitable.

Wheelchair Beautician

by Charles Mathis

If you've got the right aptitude, running a beauty shop can be a real moneymaker, even if you're in a wheelchair.

Jo Cooley is proof of that.

She's got what it takes: artistic ability, a keen business mind, a love of people and a fighting spirit that gives in to no adversity.

"When it comes to running a beauty service," she says, "I don't see a bit of difference between a handicapped person and an able-bodied one."

Any type of business that can be conducted while sitting down, Jo believes, can be a money making proposition for handicapped persons with talent and determination enough to "convince the customer."

At Mayfair Beauty Shoppe in downtown Mocksville, N.C., Jo, a vibrant 56, has been convincing patrons from a wheelchair for 30 years.

"I have done as many as 22 heads in a day," she says. "My customers don't even consider that I'm handicapped."

How does she do it?

Besides sheer determination, she has only two gimmicks—a slipper chair and a low shampoo bowl.

To enable her to reach the shampoo bowl and to wash hair with ease, she simply had the sink lowered about a foot.

The slipper chair is an antique from the time when beds were so high up that a small chair, to step on to climb in bed, was a handy

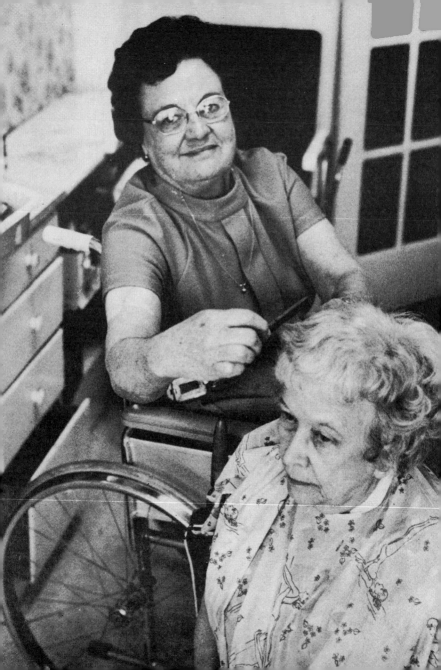

thing to have. Not to be confused with the shampoo chair, it is located in a room separate from the shampoo area and has a seat less than 12 inches from the floor. This permits the person whose hair is being worked on to be lower than Jo's wheelchair.

"You've got to build up a platform for you to be higher than your customer. Either that or get you a chair that's much lower than the one you're in," she says. "I tried everything, even a piano stool, but I found that a slipper chair is the most practicable."

Jo, who has four operators, believes that the high cost of living makes it impossible for a one-operator beauty shop to make much more than expenses. "To make money in this day and time you've got to have operators. You've got to keep your overhead down as much as you can."

How much money is required to open a beauty business?

"With supplies, equipment and plumbing," she says, "it would take close to $5,000 at least. You have to have air conditioning, dryers, booths, wiring—you'd do well to get it for that. I bought my shop 33 years ago for $800, but I'll spend more than that this year redecorating."

Through the years, Jo has made enough money to keep two wheelchairs in operating condition, to maintain specially-equipped automobiles, to erect an apartment building and to play the stock market.

She admits to making as much money on the stock market as in her beauty shop. Her advice for others who'd like to try it: "Get you a good broker, but don't listen to him too much."

She advises against trying to operate a beauty shop at home. "You won't have any privacy and people will expect you to work all kinds of hours."

Here's some Cooley pointers for those thinking about entering the beauty business:

• Find a good low-rent location where there's a lot of walking traffic.

• Minimize your disability and listen to the troubles of your customers.

• Be better than your competitors.

• Keep up with the changing hair styles. Take all the training you can possibly get.

• Never try to build your business on sympathy.

• Remember that the main thing is to make the customer look pretty, which often will give her as much a lift as going to the doctor.

• Also remember that it takes several years to build up a business, "no matter how good you are."

It was an automobile accident in 1942 that resulted in Jo being paralyzed from the waist down. She was 26 at the time and a beautician with three-years experience. The doctors were certain she wouldn't be around long, seven years at the most, and members of her family tried their best to talk her into selling her shop and taking it easy for the rest of her life.

But she couldn't be persuaded.

Jo drives her own car equipped with hand controls.

Personal independence was just too important.

"I couldn't exist being on the receiving line all the time," she says. "I've got to feel that I am leading a useful life. I've got to contribute."

She not only runs a business, rents apartments and plays the stocks but also "works out" three afternoons a week by pedaling a bicycle machine by hand in the physical therapy department at Wake Forest University; takes a great deal of pleasure in visiting other handicapped persons, especially when they're new to their dilemma and in need of a pep talk; speaks to civic clubs throughout the state; and serves on the area Easter Seal Society board and on

the Governor's Study Committee for Architectural Barriers.

Thanks to Jo's persuasiveness, Mocksville is equipped with rampways and cut out curbings, making it possible for persons in wheelchairs to go about their business whether it be in courthouse, department store or library.

"Mocksville is the most architecturally barrier-free town I know of," she smiles. "Even the jail is accessible."

Since the first rampways were built, Jo pointed out, it has been found that they can sometimes cause a drainage problem and that cutting a space in the curbing can often be much simpler and serve the purpose just as well.

Jo founded the North Carolina Paraplegia Association and served as its president for five years. Through efforts by her and her fellow association members, the Building Code of North Carolina in 1967 made a ruling that all new public buildings must be accessible to persons in wheelchairs.

In 1970, she was recipient of the North Carolina Handicapped Citizen of the Year Award and was invited to address both houses of the North Carolina legislature.

She carried no notes, just spoke from her heart about the need for making buildings accessible to persons in wheelchairs and about how difficult it is for a traveling handicapped person to locate a restroom.

"Happiness," she told them, "is finding a bathroom door big enough to scoot your wheelchair through."

Investment Management

Courage and science helped Tom Rogers, totally paralyzed by polio, to rebuild his career.

By William Clark

Young Tom Rogers is in business for himself.

Thereby hangs a tale—and a heartwarming and inspiring one it is.

The letterhead of Tom's office stationery reads Thomas Rogers Company, Investments. From 1959 until earlier this year, Tom worked for Waddell & Reed as a mutual fund salesman. Now, with his own firm, this enterprising 32-year-old can and does handle not only funds, but the full line of listed and over-the-counter securities.

Tom is paralyzed from the neck down.

Monumental courage and determination, the loving care and good sense of devoted parents, and the remarkable ingenuity of communications engineers are all part of the Tom Rogers story. His invasion of the investment business has been in many ways a family adventure conducted in an atmosphere of affection and high good humor. But,

make no mistake about it, Tom is a sharp, no-nonsense broker, and he's making money at it.

Tom had completed his freshman year at Cornell university when polio struck. There followed long months and years of iron lungs and immobility, then inch-by-inch improvement, under the supervision of a uniquely optimistic and determined therapist, to his present condition.

Breathing is not an involuntary function with Tom. He must consciously and continuously work to do it, but he does so all day long without artificial aids. At night he sleeps in a motorized bed that rocks, the rocking action being sufficient to induce breathing until he awakes.

Turned to Investing

Tom's father, Howard, is a retired manufacturer of heavy machinery, and Tom had thought about engineering as a career before his illness. Afterward, as he

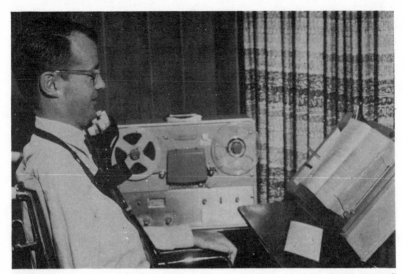

Thomas Rogers, Moline, demonstrates "collar," designed for him by Illinois Bell Telephone Company, which permits him to operate investment business despite the fact that he is a polio victim. By punching various buttons on collar with his chin, Rogers can operate telephones, tape recorder, and page turner.

reached the point where he could be pushed about in a wheelchair and as his own remarkable spirit enabled him to consider things other than his own survival, his interest turned to law and investing. The latter was not surprising in view of the activities of his uncle, Sampson Rogers, Jr., Chicago, a partner in McMaster Hutchinson & Co.

Without indulging in dramatics over the courage and effort required, let it be recorded that as Tom embarks on his own investment business he also has completed three years of study toward a degree in law.

Now, how does a fine-looking young man accomplish all this when

he is unable to move from the neck down? He begins by being equipped with a set of parents like Howard and Helen Rogers.

Use Mechanical Hoists

Tom works and sleeps in an addition built to the Rogers house in a rolling, wooded section of his city. Mechanical hoists are used to transfer him to bed or chair or automobile. Off his room is what appears to be a large closet with books lining the wall and an astonishingly clutter-free floor. Closer inspection, however, shows that the "books" are painted on the wall (by artist Helen) and the floor is clear because it is an elevator that takes

Tom—or anybody else—down to the basement.

In the basement, among other things, is assorted apparatus used in exercising Tom, a workshop operated by Howard, and an attractively finished room where Tom occasionally conducts investment club meetings. He and two friends organized one in 1957 and there now are 21 members.

On the basement wall at the bottom of the elevator shaft is an inviting line-up of wine barrels—also painted by Mrs. Rogers. "You gotta keep moving around here or you'll get painted," Tom warned.

Key Device

The key device that makes the business possible is a collar with nine buttons which Tom can push with his chin. Designed by Illinois Bell Telephone Company Engineer James Smith, with Gale Knittle assisting, the collar enables Tom to perform a variety of chores.

One button operates a page turner, an ingenious contrivance which, each time it's activated reels in thread clipped to a book page just enough to turn the page. Two buttons work telephones. Tom can hold one call while taking another, if he wishes, and can summon an operator at will. He speaks into a mouthpiece built into the collar.

Four buttons do various things about a tape recorder—start, stop, record, replay, and so on. By another arrangement it is possible for Tom to cut to a specific message that may have been recorded from a phone call in his absence.

Can Be Alone

Two of the nine buttons on the collar don't do anything yet, but the way things are going Tom'll think of something.

The collar makes it possible for him to initiate communication with anybody and this, in turn, makes it possible for him to be alone more than at any other time in many years.

Tom does most of his business in the afternoon and evening. He's still a great believer in mutual funds and handles business in this area directly. Transactions in listed and over-the-counter securities are channeled through McMaster Hutchinson. If it is necessary for him to sign a document, he takes pen in mouth (with the help of a mouthpiece devised by his mother) to do so.

Seeking Best Potential

As noted, Tom is three-fourths of the way along on a study program leading to a bar examination.

"Law would be good," he said. "I like taxes and estate planning, but it seems just a little dry compared with the market. I'm trying to discover at this point where the best potential is. I guess my view of law is somewhat changed by the fact that I seem to be making out as a broker."

Lawyer or broker, butcher or baker, Tom will make out.

William Clark is Financial Editor of the Chicago Tribune, which granted permission to reprint this outstanding story.

CBSA owner and operator Harry Hughes is making copies for the 3M designed advertising light boxes. He is paralyzed from the waist down as the result of an auto accident.

This new program of CBSA centers could provide the answer you have been looking for and provide you with a good income.

Copy Shop, Sign Making, Addressing

Independently owned and operated by handicapped individuals, the Community Business Services Associates (CBSA)* centers are a central service within a community that makes various copying services available to the general public.

These services include making copies, addressing lists, laminating services, statement-making systems, point-of-display advertising systems, salesmen's prospecting systems and short-run duplication services.

The needs for these services have been demonstrated in pilot centers by the founders and developers of CBSA, the Minnesota Mining and Manufacturing Company (3M).

How the program works

A properly selected and trained individual in a properly selected location should be able to, with the material prepared by 3M, maintain

*This program no longer exists. However, a copy business is still very much an occupational alternative for some disabled individuals.

a successful and profitable CBSA center. His net income should be equal to, or greater than, the average income of the community and of course there is the always present possibility for much greater earnings.

To date, all CBSA centers are owned and operated independently by individuals who are physically incapacitated to a point where they were considered unemployable. Many were even on public assistance programs. These individuals were referred to the 3M company by the Division of Vocational Rehabilitation of the state wherein the individual lived. After a selection and screening process, the ownership and establishment of a CBSA center became a part of the rehabilitation plan for the individual.

With the help of the local DVR counselor, a survey of the community is made and a meeting of community leaders is held to determine the quality and quantity of community support. If all other fac-

Hughes, a college graduate, finds that his ability to type is a real asset to the operation of his business.

tors are positive, the plan is put into effect. This involves the training of the owner and operator in the use of the equipment, the function and sale of the applications, and assistance to the owner in the over-all establishment of the business. It is necessary for the owner to do a considerable amount of reading, studying, and he must pass a specially prepared training course. The course is completed when the owner is certified as having passed the essential items necessary for success in operating a copy service center. The course includes several days of on-the-job training with a 3M representative. Constant follow up is maintained between 3M and the CBSA center owner through the use of a monthly publication and through an association of CBSA owners and operators.

Individuals interested in qualifying to be a CBSA owner should have enough finger and arm dexterity to operate the copy equipment and, hopefully, a typewriter. In some cases, if the owner is only

able to sell the services and do the so-called contact work, a back-up member of his family can do the actual production work. In some cases, mentally retarded individuals have been profitably employed by CBSA owners to do production work under their supervision.

One important feature of an owner is that he must be willing

Harry Hughes is visited often by Joseph Kelly, counselor for the Wisconsin State Board of Vocational and Adult Education.

to make calls, meet the public, and sell new, unique, and creative ideas. CBSA centers are manned by quadriplegics, paraplegics, and hemiplegics very successfully, many being operated from homes.

What's in a CBSA center package?

A typical inventory of equipment and supplies includes: one dry photo-copier, one Thermo-Fax copier, one portable overhead projector, 15 advertising display light boxes, a supply of materials for the equipment, a complete training course, a complete system of accounting for the center, personal training and assistance, and a national sales effort on the part of the 3M company.

Looking into the future

The 3M companies, highly respected and a multi-million dollar operation, have taken a bold new step into the future with this program designed to provide respectable employment for qualified persons who have a disability. CBSA owner Olive Holz, in Kewanee, Illinois, said, "The sky is the limit if one has the determination and initiative and drive to get there. I think it is wonderful that there are so many opportunities now for us."

Accounting

From an office in his home, Herbert K. Gass doesn't let Frederick's Ataxia bar him from being an accountant for the town of Deerfield, Mass. He also handles general and tax accounting for several businesses and individuals.

Each student receives a valuable set of watch makers tools, including the finest and latest equipment. Cost is born by the sponsoring agency or, in some cases, by the student.

Learn Watch Repair

TUITION is free to all students at this Joseph Bulova School of Watchmaking.

Arde Bulova, the founder, said, "No one understands the value of time better than a disabled person. Each second and each minute gain new dimensions."

Watch repair can be a very rewarding business for there is a continuous demand for quality workmanship to maintain the accuracy of the many clocks and watches assuring every well trained craftsman a secure livelihood.

According to Benjamin H. Lipton, Director, students today upon graduation, receive from $55 to $85 a week as a starting salary. Most of the graduates are today earning a full living, however, it is important to point out that many of them, upon entering business required a good many months before they became self-sufficient. Total weekly earnings are only limited by the individual's own imagination.

Costs include those tools and supplies which will run about $500 and of course, monthly housing costs. An estimated breakdown is as follows:

Room	$ 40
Board	65
Personal Laundry	5
Incidentals	10
Total	$120

There is a dormitory that has the lower floor planned to accommodate wheelchair students and the latest equipment and facilities have been provided to make even the seriously disabled person comfortable during their stay at this school. The upper floor has been designed to accommodate disabled students who do not require the use of a wheelchair. Every room is individually air-conditioned and daily maid service is provided.

The average day's schedule for each student may vary since some

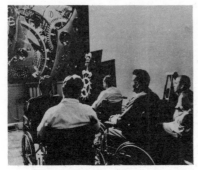

A special series of sound and color training films have been devised and produced by the school.

may be on a limited work tolerance, of a four hour day and others on a full six hour day. During the time that the student is at school he undergoes studies in practical work in the course. Those students that require attention in the medical department may arrange that during their daily schedule. Students that require regular treatment, either in

the school or outside, may arrange it so that it runs concurrently with the course and does not impeed progress of the individual.

A new student can be admitted in the first week of any month and the average time to complete the full course is 18 to 20 months. Although there is a short waiting list at the present time a qualified applicant will have to wait only 6 to 8 weeks before being admitted.

The Joseph Bulova School of Watchmaking admits the disabled. both veterans and civilians. Only in special instances does the school accept applications from non-handicapped persons. The course is divided into eight basic training sections, each section is taught by a specialist in that particular skill; preliminary training, balance work, lathe work, hairspring work, assembly, escapement theory and matching, finishing, general repairs.

J. H. Jones, G. M. Romunstad, W. H. Higdon, three graduates of the Bulova school now own and operate, very successfully, the "Jewel Box".

Good Wage Possible In Watch Repair

A nationwide survey of graduates of a 22-year-old institution dedicated to the training of the physically handicapped indicates that, today in America, disabled persons can and do hold normal jobs and receive normal wages and salaries. Nearly 500 of the 907 graduates of the Joseph Bulova School of Watchmaking responded to a survey questionnaire, according to school director Benjamin H. Lipton. Replies from 41 states show that median weekly work income ranges from $96.40 to $135.76, and that individual work ranged from $50 to $400 a week. Median weekly work income for all graduates responding was $116.36.

Training Is Key

"A disabled person who receives adequate training can find and, more important, hold a productive job today in our technological society," Mr. Lipton said. "That is shown very clearly by the statistics in the survey. The statistics indicate that a physically handicapped person who does *not* receive proper training cannot participate productively in our society. Training is the answer to physical disability."

Mr. Lipton states that the Bulova School offers two types of tuition-free courses for the disabled: a watch repair course that graduates qualified watchmakers; and a precision instrument course that graduates qualified instrument specialists. The courses have led to employment in the watch manufacturing and precision-instrument industries; employment as a watchmaker; self-employment at home as a watchmaker; employment as an instructor in industrial, vocational or watchmaking schools; and to the creation, operation and ownership of watchmaking businesses in the service and retail areas.

"These are very encouraging results when we consider that 20 years ago doubters viewed physical rehabilitation work as a strictly charitable endeavor," said Lipton.

Limited To Home

"Our graduates have proved that the physically handicapped person can compete productively with the non-disabled person," he said, "even in those cases where physical disabilities are so crippling as to permit work only in the home—outside the normal competitive employment area."

The watch repair course graduates who can work only in their homes, he added, have the lowest median weekly income, $96.40. This compares to a weekly median income of $124.22 for watch repair graduates who are store owner-operators, and to a medium weekly income of $101.28 for precision instrument course graduates who are employed in industry. The relatively low weekly income of precision instrument graduates probably is explained by the fact that the Bulova School has offered a precision instrument course only since 1957. The course had its first graduate in 1958, whereas the watch repair course has been producing graduates since 1946. Consequently, watch repair graduates include persons with the longest employment records.

Some Unemployed

Not all the graduates who responded are productively employed. Four are unemployed and seeking work; 14 are unable to work because of illness due to their physical disabilities; and eight have retired. The graduates of the school were categorized by Mr. Lipton according to disability types. These types include: paraplegia, pulmonary tuberculosis; miscellaneous war-inflicted wounds; fractures; amputation of the lower extremities; cardiac disease; back injuries; poliomyelitis; internal disorders such as liver ailments, gastrointestinal ailments, and kidney ailments; arthritis, neuro-psychiatric disabilities; peripheral vascular disease; congenital deformities; and deafness and partial deafness.

Job Titles

Job titles for watch repair course graduates included: watch repairman; clock repairman; watch and jewelry salesman; repairs department manager; merchandising manager; production manager; and jewelry store proprietor. Job titles for precision instrument course graduates included: electro-mechical assembler; instrument technician; calibration repair specialist; mechanical inspector; electrician; electrical repairman; supervisor; and foreman.

Other types of occupations listed by the graduates include aircraft instrument repairman; instrument maker, time lock inspector, inertial instrument evaluation specialist, field technician of missiles, solderer, model maker, and lathe operator.

More information on this school can be obtained by writing: Benjamin H. Lipton, Director; Joseph Bulova School of Watchmaking; 40-24 62nd Street; Woodside, Long Island, New York.

Reweaving

Another idea for a home operated business is reweaving. Repairing damaged clothes can be a profitable service-oriented business. One company which caters to the homebound reweaver is Fabricon Company, 2021 Montrose Avenue, Chicago, IL 60618. This company offers a course which enables disabled persons to set up their own business.

Lurner Williams, probably the best-known sports reporter in South Georgia, covers games over a wide area. He also does many feature articles. "Interviewing Miss Georgia of 1960 is one of the many pleasures in being a newspaper reporter."

Lurner Williams, journalist, says, "My life is full—because I chose it that way!"

Newspaper Reporter

For centuries man had run a mile to see who could come *closest* to running the distance in four minutes. Then in 1956 Roger Bannister, of England, ran a mile in *less* than four minutes. Since then it has been done time and time again. Why? Someone proved it could be done. No longer is there a mental barrier to confront!

"Man is made but little lower than the angels, and God has crowned him with glory and honor. The Apostle Paul said, 'I can do *all* things—through Christ, which strengtheneth me'," so says 33 year old Lurner Williams who can bend neither hips nor knees because of the after effects of arthritis. Stricken with rheumatic fever on January 5, 1941, he was confined to bed. He was in the seventh grade and has not been able to return to school—except on a stretcher—since. Hospitalization for long periods followed as did other attacks. Surgery helped his hips a little so now he can sit up slightly. It is in this position he does his work, typing with speeds 70 to 75 words per minute.

At age 21, Lurner was dismissed from the hospital, but not before spending four months taking an intensified course in English, spelling and typing. An Elks auxiliary donated a used typewriter and his career was started.

"I handled magazine subscriptions and sold Christmas cards, addressed postal cards for baby showers and anything else I could get. My home is in a village of 250 people in a farming community and the only other town is twelve miles away, with a population of just 2,500 people."

Lurner's winning smile and personality won him many new friends. The County Grand Jury appointed him Notary Public and ex-officio Justice of the Peace. "It was a slow take-off for a business, but people were cooperating and I knew I had to work and keep pushing. I made a little money that first year

The jacket Lurner wears was awarded him by the Jeff Davis High School teams after he stayed with both boys and girls through the state tournament, lending encouragement and inspiration. Both teams won state title in unprecedented fashion.

with all the business combined and I was encouraged greatly."

Not standing still, he began a correspondence course in accounting and then the next year began to help people in preparing their income tax returns. Barber shops can be an excellent advertising medium —three barber shops in the county seat passed the word around and he found some people driving from twelve miles away to obtain his services. "I gave each unreserved attention and time."

Lurner kept working. He completed his high school work at home and in June, 1950, at the age of 23, "I entered the first high school building in my life, being rolled in on a stretcher, where I received my high school diploma."

"I had been serving as correspondent for the local paper for years, and branched out to the Savannah Morning News—a daily. I contacted the Atlanta Journal, which covers Dixie like the dew', but they wrote they could not use me as correspondent because I did not live in the county seat. I wrote again and they gave me the same reply. So I began sending in news items. They were unsolicited—and unused for twelve weeks—but on the 13th week, they used one of my items! Each month since then I have gotten a check from the Atlanta Journal."

"In November, 1956, I made a discovery, learning that a station wagon could be equipped as an ambulance. I bought a 1955 Ford station wagon and from then on I was a 'roving' reporter. But in fairness to, and appreciation of, my tax clients, I stay home day and night from January 15 through April 15, with the exception of about five or six nights—and tournament time. I built a home with an office in early 1958 on the highway. I travel more than 20,000 miles each year in my wagon—a 1959 Ford now.

"I have had an opportunity to give testimony in more than 65 churches in this part of the state. While I have spoken from many passages in the Bible, I have tried to impress one thing—man's potential is limitless. Positive thinking can create miracles! Whatever I have accomplished, little as it may be, came as the result of wanting to do it and believing I could do it. I discard negative thoughts and concentrate only on the positive. I belong to the Lions Club and the Junior Chamber of Commerce. I assume the same positions of responsibility in the club as the other members and want no favors. Some of the members can do things I cannot do, and I can do things some of them cannot, so things even up!

"I shall not conclude without a word about a dear, devoted 72-year-old mother who has been my nurse, cook, secretary and booster, all these years."

How does he do it? Lurner says, with deep humility, "All this has come to pass because of one simple thing: I made an effort because people helped me so much, and people helped me so much because I made an effort!"

A Setup For A Handicapped Writer

by JERRY CONGER

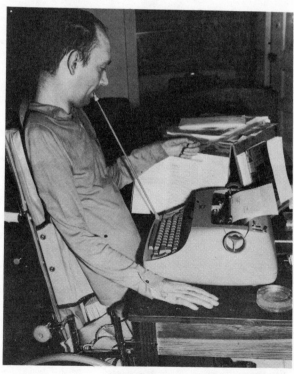

Jerry Conger is making money selling articles to magazines. His work is made much easier with his revolving bookstand, eraser-tipped mouthstick and electric typewriter.

My recent sale of an article to a national magazine, and the provisional placement of two more, rewarded a long apprenticeship and a longer struggle to be a writer. Perhaps the most satisfying reward came from knowing I did the research and writing independently — although I am a quadriplegic. But most importantly, my set-up

A revolving bookstand set me free. My idea, executed in plywood by a skilled carpenter, held four books. Applying light pressure with either my relatively strong left arm or the mouthstick, I could easily revolve it on its lazy Susan. There was one problem: the paper carriage wouldn't return if the bookstand was placed in the ideal

This bookstand, revolving on its own Lazy Susan, holds four reference books, plus paper and envelope supplies — all within easy reach.

of desk, typewriter, and bookstand (or the principles involved) could serve the needs of other handicapped persons.

At first, the solutions to my problem looked simple: a mouthstick and an electric typewriter. I had a 40x28-inch desk built and discovered that I'd inadequately defined the problem. Sure, I could peck the keys with my mouthstick, by writing entails more than that. Research lays the groundwork of all good writing. At the very least, a dictionary and thesaurus must be at hand. My hands, however, proved less than functional for handling books and papers.

spot — just to the left of the typewriter. For this reason, only one typewriter would serve: IBM's Selectric, which has no paper carriage. Now with all these tools, I could do research, make notes, and prepare my manuscripts.

But this wasn't the limit of the bookstand's utility. The openings between the sides provided storage space for envelopes, postage, correspondence, and manuscripts. Beyond this, I learned to snag envelopes and papers with the mouthstick, slide them toward me, and secure them between mouthstick and hand. In time, with practice and patience, I began to insert paper and envelopes in the typewriter — something I'd scarcely thought possible. Today, I wouldn't be afraid to challenge a good secretary to a race because I seldom fail to line up the paper straight the first time. The feat requires little use of hands and shoulders (fortunately for me). I also became adept at making erasures with my eraser-tipped mouthstick.

The principle of the bookstand can be extended to serve other needs. It could be built to other dimensions for the unique problems of other people. For example, it might be modified for a handicapped painter. Or it might be used for reading and other recreation.

The set-up of desk, typewriter, and bookstand could solve a universal problem among the severely handicapped: the difficulty of communicating. Although all won't wish to write professionally, they do need to correspond with friends and relatives, and answer business letters.

For me, the set-up means the difference between non-productivity and creativity. Dictation is out of the question. The creative juices just won't flow unless I can set my own words to paper, a peculiarity many writers share. And there's this important point to remember: the personal satisfaction of doing one's own work is a universally-recognized component of good adjustment.

Book Writing

Worried because she was unable to work and help in the support of her Amish family, Leah I. Schwartz, a 25-year-old woman who must use a wheelchair as a result of muscular dystrophy, decided that one way she could earn some money was to compile a cookbook of Amish food. (ED NOTE: Although Amish persons object to having photographs taken of them, Miss Schwartz consented to this portrait being used as it appears on her cookbook.)

KOOM - ESSE
(COME EAT)

AN
AMISH
COOKBOOK
BY LEAH I. SCHWARTZ

Christmas Tree Farming

Running a business from a wheelchair requires a blend of courage, faith and dogged determination rarely found outside the ranks of the handicapped. It took all three of those ingredients, plus a generous helping of imagination, to make a going concern of Bob's Yuletide Forest, a unique "choose and cut" Christmas tree plantation near Modesto, California.

Robert Jorgensen, the young cerebal palsy victim who owns the venture, thinks it is a success story that might be repeated by other handicapped persons.

His first experiment involved a planting of 500 seedlings of several varieties, a half dozen of which seemed to do well in the San Joaquin Valley heat. Traditional Yule trees did not fare well, so he turned his attention to less well-known varieties, subjecting the trees to irrigation, weed and pest control, and careful pruning.

"In the beginning I was pretty much on my own," Jorgensen says. "No-one knew much then about growing Christmas trees in hot climates, and I made some mistakes." One such mistake was planting several hundred trees on marginal river-bottom land which was subject to frequent flooding. Only 30 or so trees survived and they were taken one night by thieves.

Jorgensen took the difficulties in stride. Like handicapped people everywhere, he had learned years earlier not to become discouraged by temporary setbacks. As a youngster, he had been a member of the Boy Scouts of America, achieving the rank of Life Scout in a special troop for handicapped boys. But because of the physical requirements, he was not eligible to move on to the Eagle ranking. Instead, he launched into an intensive one-year study and service program which resulted in his receiving the

Chicken Farming

After a spinal cord injury paralyzed him from the waist down, Howard Alexander built a two-story chicken house, with a ramp to the second floor, and went into the poultry business. To feed the 3,000 broilers he raises at a time, he picks up 100-pound feed bags, places them on his lap and wheels them around to the feeders. The Kentuckian also dresses the chickens and prepares them for market.

Colorful bumper stickers are part of Jorgensen's ongoing promotional program to advertise his business.

prestigious God and Country Award.

Graduating in the top five per cent of his high school class, he went on to study agriculture at a nearby community college. That is where he began the search for a business that could be run from a wheelchair, a search that led finally to the tree farm.

"The first problem, of course, was figuring out a way to give myself some mobility," Jorgensen says. That was solved simply enough by purchasing a used electric golf cart.

The other tools of his trade consist of a flocking machine and an assortment of ordinary pruning shears. Automated electric shears are available for persons who have difficulty with the manual equipment. As an extra promotional attraction for the business, Jorgensen and his father have constructed a miniature railroad which offers children rides through the forest during December.

Do tree plantations offer pos-sible income opportunities for other handicapped people? Jorgensen thinks they might.

"To give you some idea of the income potential: I have about 4,000 trees on three acres. With trees reaching sale size in four years or less, there is a potential 1,000 sales per year at an average of $5-$6 per tree. I spend from five to twenty hours a week work-in the forest and hire help during certain times of the year. So, some quick figuring will show I'm not getting rich, but if a person could manage a larger acreage, income should rise accordingly. Besides, there are some pretty great side benefits, especially when the forest is full of happy families during those weekends in December.

"Many people are surprised to see me running the business," Jorgensen says. 'But no one comes to buy a tree because it was grown by a handicapped person; and I'm sure no one stays away for that reason either."

•While parents shop for trees, children get free rides through the forest on miniature railroad built by Jorgensen with the help of his father.

Blind Farmer Raises Chickens

JOE JONES, SIGHTLESS FOR 16 YEARS—MAINTAINS AN EFFICIENT, PROFITABLE BROILER OPERATION.

by A. B. Kennerly

Paul Darden is showing his neighbors around Linden, Texas that, no matter what the handicap, any person can become successful if he has a constructive attitude and the patience to stay with his convictions. Darden can speak convincingly, for he is totally blind.

Darden became blind in 1945, and this catastrophe seemingly put an end to his ambitions to go into the poultry business. He spent many years making the adjustment. But always dominating his lonely thoughts was the crushed desire to live and work with poultry. Then,

one morning he decided to make the plunge. He visited his county agent, Truitt Powell, who listened sympathetically to Darden's ideas.

Now the Agricultural Extension Service, which operates in all states on a cooperative plan uniting the efforts of the county, state and federal government, is dedicated to the task of helping people to help themselves., County Extension agents do nothing for the person or group that these people can do for themselves.

Darden offered the county agent a distinct challenge, for what could a blind man do for himself in the poultry business? Never-the-less, Powell accepted the challenge and agreed that he would go along with the man to the extent that he was willing to help himself.

Today, Powell is enthusiastic about the tremendous progress the poultryman has made, and Darden

himself can scarcely realize that he is a full-fledged broiler grower turning out 80,000 pounds of broiler meat a year. This is soon to be doubled as Darden completes the second house.

From the beginning, Powell encouraged Darden to do everything he could for himself. Because the county agent had many contacts who could be helpful to the blind poultryman, he himself made most of the contacts. Otherwise, Darden did most of the other chores including building the poultry house.

Quietly, Powell talked with some of the merchants on the county courthouse square who gave $300 toward expenses. The Rural Electric Administration in the county donated some poles for use in house construction. A sawmill operator donated some lumber. This was to give Darden a start on his longed-for poultry establishment. It

Darden feels for the switch that will turn on the motor that turns the feed auger. He buys feed in bulk, augers it into the cart and distributes it to the hungry chickens. Later purchases will include automatic feeders which will carry feed to the troughs in the poultry house.

was about this time that Powell had a chance to realize with what earnestness Darden was tackling the task.

A neighbor passing the Darden home near midnight heard a faint thumping of the earth. He paused long enough to stroll down where Darden was working on the building site. Lining up the posts, he was staking them off and digging the post holes.

"Why are you working at night? the neighbor asked. "Why don't you do that in the daytime?"

Darden rested an instant on the post-hole digger. "Oh, I can see just as well at night as in the day-time."

Oops! Darden discovers he has lost a couple of chicks. Dead chicks are picked up and destroyed, but the poultryman has a very low death loss.

While he was building the sceptic tank, Darden found himself at one of the infrequent occasions when he had to call for outside help. He went over to a neighbor and asked him how to cut a certain angle in the material. The neighbor not only was happy to explain how but told Darden he would go over the next morning and cut the material. By the time the neighbor could get over there, Darden had cut the material and had it nailed in place.

Meanwhile, Powell was doing some of the things for Darden which he could not do for himself. He was advising on the best construction of the poultry house that would add to profits later on. He helped make arrangements with a feed company to provide feed, chicks and medication when the building was finished. Darden had planned to raise laying hens in cages, but since it was too late that season to start, Powell advised him to raise a house of broilers. He could convert the house to laying cages later.

However, Darden was so keen to make a success of the venture, he led all 20 of the other growers who were financed by the feed dealer. He was able to produce 44 pounds of broilers on 100 pounds of feed, an accomplishment many other broiler growers would like to duplicate. With this encouragement, he decided he would stay with broilers.

The house he built would hold 6,000 broilers, so he talked with Powell about the feasibility of building another house to double the capacity. The poultryman was making good progress. He had made arrangements to buy the equipment he needed such as brooders, feeders and waterers; a banker and the equipment dealer going on his note. Darden figures to have these paid off by the fall of 1961.

The FHA is financing the construction of the second house on a Title 1 loan. Darden is making arrangements to buy more equipment, putting in automatic waterers and feeders. These, he figures will be paid for in 1964 if plans go as scheduled. Powell, with the resources of Texas A&M College supporting him, is able to advise the poultryman the best profit-making and debt-paying methods of raising broilers. Darden puts these ideas to work and comes up with good gains on his broilers.

The feed dealer who is sponsoring the broiler grower pays Darden 2 cents per pound for his labor, buildings and equipment. The dealer provides the day-old chicks, feed and medication.

As Darden gained new confidence in his abilities, Powell suggested other activities that would reduce the food bill. He arranged for a heifer calf for Darden to raise for a milk cow. He arranged for some pigs for pork. The home garden supplies fresh vegetables for eating fresh and for freezing.

"I'm going stronger than ever," Darden almost shouts his enthusiasm for his work. "For the first time in many years I can see a wonderful future ahead."

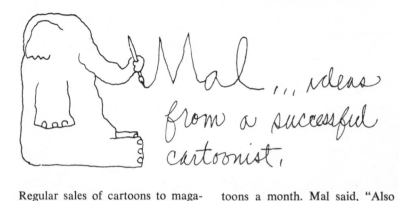

Mal ... ideas from a successful cartoonist,

Regular sales of cartoons to magazines like New Yorker, Playboy, TV Guide, Saturday Review, and some twenty-five others gives Malcolm Hancock an income well into five figures.

Mal, as he signs his work, was glad to tell how he got started and to offer suggestions that might help other ACCENT readers who might like to give cartooning a try.

He became a paraplegic, L-2, at 17 when he fell off a cliff in the Wisconsin Dells in 1953. Mal and his wife, Mary, who he married in 1961, have a 12-year-old daughter.

Two years of commercial art at Denver University got Mal started in art. Then, when pressure sores forced him to go into a hospital he started doing cartoons about hospital life for other patients. When his ideas were accepted enthusiastically he decided to start concentrating on cartooning and enrolled in a Famous Artists course by mail.

Later, while working as a layout artist for a food and drug chain, he made his first sales to some magazines, no longer published, that were buying some 200 cartoons a month. Mal said, "Also I immediately started sending to the big magazines and I immediately started getting rejection slips." At the same time he began submitting to several specific markets to find out from where the best response to his cartoons came.

Finally his first big sale came when the Saturday Evening Post liked an idea and bought it.

Mal suggests that beginning cartoonists start by submitting to smaller magazines, always keeping in mind the slant being used by various types of magazines. He usually sends a batch of eight cartoons done on 8½ x 11 white paper to each publication and, when he was getting started, tried to get out at least three batches a week. "Then, when they are returned, get them right back out again to other publishers," he says.

Who is best judge of talent?

Friends and art teachers can give you an idea, but the best judges of your work are the editors who pay the money for what they like. Package your cartoons (always include a stamped self-addressed envelope if you want them returned) and start sending them out. And remember, try a variety of markets.

"Cartooning can be fun and very rewarding and it doesn't cost much to get started," says Mal. "It took a while to develop the style I use now, but my present style evolved as I went along and the business has been very good to me."· →

"You can't create in a vacuum," says Mal. He tape records such things as lectures, educational courses on TV, political speeches, to provide a continuing source of ideas.

CARTOONS BY *Mal*

PLAYBOY

"If you're not making these long-distance calls to Australia, then who is?"

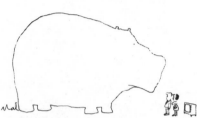

'Don't argue with him, dear . . . turn on *Wild Kingdom*.'

TV GUIDE

'Believe me, J.B., it will be an entirely new concept in Westerns.'

Saturday Review **World**

"Maybe our problem is too many chiefs."

After an auto accident Glen Fowler took a correspondence course in art and is

Building New Careers For Himself And Other Artists

by Keith Hodgdon

Glen Fowler uses a brush held in his mouth to produce pictures with exquisite detail.

At seventeen, Glen Fowler faced a bleak future — no job and no direction. He'd just broken his neck in an auto accident, and as yet he hadn't a hint of the bright promise in the art business that lay ahead.

When first injured in 1951, Glen was by no means an artist. He had started taking art lessons at fourteen, so while he lay in the hospital awaiting rehabilitation he found his fascination with shape, perspective and color flashing mental images on the screen of his mind. He knew that it meant nothing in practical terms unless he could put those images to canvas and sell them, so he worked out a pencil-in-the-mouth technique.

Then he tried a brush and canvas. Enough raw talent was obvious to a representative of the Famous Artists Schools in Westport, Conn., so that in 1957 he offered Glen a three-year commercial art course as a scholarship. It's a correspondence course with periodic tests on the study material mailed to the school where they're corrected, graded and pictorially commented on by artist-instructors.

Glen blossomed as an artist. He explains, "Their course helped me to improve my work to a point where I could now sell it." Long before he finished he had, on his own, won several prizes and sold enough paintings to encourage him to study further. Since then the school has offered Glen courses in fine art and advanced painting. A foreign association of disabled artists asked him to join them. They reproduced his work on greeting cards starting in 1962, and his earnings took a great leap forward.

In 1969 he lengthened that leap

by forming American Artists Incorporated (AAI), a group of severely disabled painters. Its purpose was to provide as many benefits to the artist as possible. For instance, AAI accepts all types of severely handicapped artists, saves artists the cost of shipping their work overseas, allows artists to retain complete ownership of their work, doesn't restrict its artists from starting or continuing their own art sales or solicitations, sends an annually audited financial statement that clearly shows what money goes where.

Winter Scene by Glen Fowler.

AAI now has twenty-eight contributing artists nationwide, and winter scenes seem to be the best sellers according to Glen, who is president and manager. The corporation is funded by a Small Business Administration direct loan under the Equal Opportunity Act, and also by sale of common stock.

AAI acts as the artists' agent in acquiring the reproduction rights of their pictures and attempting to sell them as Christmas card designs, although it hopes and plans to expand into all occasion cards and notepaper. Says Glen, "We hope someday to arrange regular art exhibits, even acquire wholesale and dealership contracts to show artists' original works and to help increase their earning power."

Glen helps the artists reach a wider audience. He says, "We send out our advertising brochures picturing our cards and allow recipients to place an order." In advertising, AAI stresses that those who buy cards will enable artists to become dignified participants in the game of life rather than mere spectators. AAI attempts to encourage others by obtaining scholarships for its artists. Their handicaps range widely — from a woman in an iron lung who paints with her mouth, to a man who paints with his foot, to a blind man who paints with imagination from dim memory.

All these painters are breaking harsh boundaries to get outside themselves. The art itself is good. Glen has no trouble in locating talented artists. Their biggest problem is one shared by every business venture, that of getting publicity and getting additional customers. American Artists Inc. is concentrating on building a reputation where it counts, in the American art market, in order to build a future bright with promise.

Ed. Note: The name AAI was later changed to Handicapped Artists of America, Inc. For information on what is currently available, write to Glen at 8 Sandy Lane, Salisbury, Mass. 01950.

They're Making Money Selling Products They Make At Home

BY EMILY SPRAGUE WURL

Pat Thomas makes over $5,000 a year from her sales through Easter Seal Homecraft Shops. She uses a wheelchair because of polio and makes all her articles in her home where she also operates a telephone answering service. Pat has three children.

Today, Patricia Thomas of Milwaukee, Wisconsin, is a very happy person, but she admits to not having always been that way. When, some years ago, polio struck and Pat became confined to a wheelchair, she was furious at her fate; complained constantly, and struck out at relatives and close friends who loved her. In Pat's words, "Expressions of sympathy seemed mere platitudes! I felt I was living in my own coffin." At that trying time in her life, Pat confesses that people around her seemed so limited. She was learning that there can be cruelty in kindness, unless accompanied by *self-help* for the individual.

Her depression ran deep until the day the teacher from the Homecraft Division of the State Vocational Rehabilitation Agency, sponsored by the Easter Seal Society, called. This teacher, by teaching her a craft, helped her attitude to change from the despair of being of no use in this world, into gradually saying, *"If I won't give up, I won't have to give up!"*

Listen to Pat today, "To bring beauty into homes by the things I make with my hands has become my chief motivation!"

Who would imagine that things of beauty could be made out of cast-offs, such as bits of felt, cloth, ribbon, sequins, smooth stones, pieces of driftwood, pine cones, even stubs of old brooms.

Pat Thomas is one of the top producers in the Homecraft Service Program.

Craft instructors, employed by the VR Division, work directly in the homes of these people whose handicaps make outside employment impossible. The training program provides an opportunity for handicapped people to learn new skills and rediscover old ones. In the early stages of training, encouragement is sometimes needed.

Even after many hours of work, the new client may not produce a salable item. Instructors then try

different methods of production or new product ideas. Each homecrafter is urged to work and produce to the limit of his ability, but little urging is needed after he receives his first check for sales from the Easter Seal Society.

All products on sale meet the high standards of workmanship set by the Homecraft Shops. Each article sells on its own merit in competititon with commercial items. Customers who purchase products do so not only because of the quality appeal of the goods, but also for the inner appeal of knowing they're helping a creative person lead a more productive life. Many sell goods directly from their homes through special orders, while others have sales outlets other than the Homecraft Shops.

Sales are made through Easter Seal Homecraft Shops located in Milwaukee, Madison, Bayfield and Appleton. The store takes no percentage of the sales and therefore

Ferdinand Lange specializes in making high quality toys for children in this shop in his home.

Ruth Brunner uses a converted room in her house to display her beautiful handpainted gift items.

is non-profit. Every penny goes to the contributor. The articles are delivered to the stores by relatives, friends, or by mail. They are kept on consignment and every sale is accounted for.

Pat's advice to those who are handicapped is to get in touch with your state's Department of Rehabilitation. If they haven't established Homecraft Shops where you live, see if you can get one started. Wisconsin might serve as a model.

Creating Christmas Cards

Grace Layton has used her outstanding artistic talents to start her own note paper and Christmas card business since having polio in 1950. She receives orders from all 48 states and Canada and employs a part-time stenographer who takes dictation and makes up orders. This fall Grace has assortments of Christmas and all occasion cards and note paper. All assortments are $1.25. Shown is one of her cards drawn with a pencil held in her mouth.

Leathercraft,
Hand Lettering,
Taking Phone Messages

By Carl C. Wood

There can be little doubt that the hands holding the telephone are the busiest hands in town. They belong to the friendliest and seemingly the happiest person in the little town of Claude, Texas. No one would question that he is also the best known individual in the entire county, and could well be voted the best loved person in the area. The well-known smiling face belongs to Tom Henry Miller.

Life began for Tom Henry the same as for most boys in the community. Then along came the cruel and crippling disease of arthritis.

Literally frozen with arthritis, Tom Henry Miller, nevertheless, has an important part in the scheme of things in a Texas town of 820 people.

For several years he was only partially disabled. His brothers used to take him to school in their little red wagon. Then at the age of nineteen, he became bedfast. For more than twenty years he has lived the days, nights, and weeks upon his bed and in this same position both day and night.

Time dragged slowly for a time. Not only the family pastor, but other ministers would often stop by to visit. It was during one of these visits that Tom Henry accepted Christ into his life. According to Tom this was the beginning of a new life. Things began to be different.

More and more folks would come by to visit. The story spread of this handsome young shut-in who, with his happy smile, could bring real happiness to those who crossed his path. He had a natural gift of doing things with his hands. With little bits of scrap leather he made little saddles by looking at the pictures in a catalogue. He also had a gift for hand lettering that was never taught at school. It was a style all his own.

One of Tom Henry's breaks came when he was asked to print the names of the charter Lion Members on a certificate which was to be framed. Because he wouldn't take any money for this job, the Lion's Club, knowing of his interest for leathercraft, bought him his first set of real tools. Miss Ida Lee Cope, an Amarillo teacher home for vacation, gave him some pointers and he was on the way to a busy life making billfolds and belts of leather. Orders started to come in. His work has now gone to foreign countries and almost every state. Since he started working with leather, everything has gone up in price, but he has refused to raise his prices. With his jolly sense of humor he says, "If my prices go up, then I'll have to pay income tax and there are too many people supporting the government as it is." However, most folks in-

On his way to church

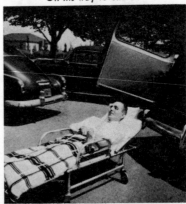

sist on paying more after they see his expert work.

After a telephone was placed by his bed, more things began to happen. Now he has two phones and he often says that there should be three. There would likely be less than a dozen people in town that he has not talked with on the phone and almost this same percentage over the countryside round about.

A year or so ago the *Claude News* offered him the job of collecting local personal news items over the phone and writing it up for the weekly edition. With this his life became still busier. Now he also writes a little weather column for the paper.

Then came the job of blowing the noon whistle and the fire alarm. Where else could you find one person who was always by his phone day and night?

Tom Henry takes subscriptions to all magazines, the *Amarillo Daily News,* and the *Amarillo Citizen.* He reports unusual news items to Radio Station KFDA. He sells greeting cards of all kinds, and he has a selection of Rawleighs supplies in his bedroom. He has charge of the community home and people come by for the key. Tom Henry takes orders for flowers for an Amarillo florist and has a better record than the store in that no one has ever failed to pay for their flowers.

Friends beat a steady path to the door of this busy person. Often one group will come before the other leaves. He loves it this way. As Tom puts it, "Even though I live in a small room, my life is the whole wide world."

Young people love to come by for a visit. Friends never tire of buying something for a gift. Most of his possessions are gifts he has received from his many friends.

Without moving anything but his arms Tom can reach his two telephones, all of the different receipt books, his order books, and news items. A TV set has brought many corners of the world into his life. It is within easy reach and the picture· is viewed in a mirror across the room. This was also a gift from friends; it was almost impossible to stop the money from coming in when this gift was started.

After the death of Tom's father a few years back, friends helped to buy a lift so his mother could move him from his bed.

Two years ago, the same brothers that carried him to school in their little red wagon worked nights to build a room on their pick-up truck so they could take him on a vacation trip to Red River, New Mexico. There he caught his first fish —also a good sun-burn.

To many of us Tom Henry will always be remembered as the one person who has meant the most to the daily scheme of things here in our quiet little town. In a contest for the busiest, the friendliest, and the most likeable person in the county, Tom Henry Miller would win hands down.

To each person who knows him, "He is the most!"

Artist Paints By Mouth

. . . *and builds a new career following tragic auto accident*

One of the most startling transformation of careers has been experienced by 33-year-old Charles Lee Smith of Knoxville, Iowa. He has known the colorless confines of coal mines where he labored in his younger years. Now, with artist's brush, he has climbed closer to heaven as he joins in the thrill of cocreating God's world, with colors more vibrant than ever seeped into the depths of a mine.

It took a tragic automobile accident, however, to bring about the transformation. It was an accident which took a heavy toll—loss of use of all Smith's facilities below his neck.

When he was introduced to the counselor from the vocational rehabilitation office three years ago, he was timidly experimenting with

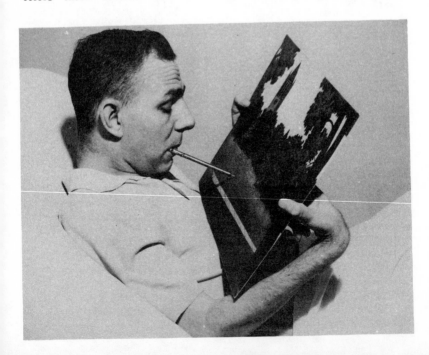

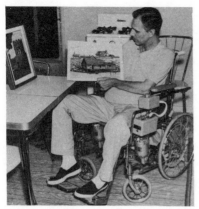

A new electric wheel chair (Everest & Jennings Standard Model) was another great step towards Smith's independence. He can now move around his home whenever he wishes.

holding a brush in his mouth while he painstakingly tried to set down on canvas the limited scenes he recollected of the Iowa countryside.

He had even dared to take the art talent test offered by The Famous Artist Schools of Westport, Connecticut. Guardedly he told his counselor that he had received confirmation on an aptitude for training in this field.

Counselor Bob Thomas had the faith and imagination to encourage Smith in this particular pursuit of a new life.

Landscapes of cornfields in autumn, covered bridges, historical landmarks—depicting the panorama which was becoming more evident to Smith's training vision—began to flow onto canvases. He tried also sketching in black and white, or with colored inks. These sketches

multiplied almost unconsciously, until he suddenly realized he had quite a variety to offer in the market place.

Sales were stimulated by a fortunate partnership with a neighboring police officer who had heard of Smith through a newspaper column. It seems that the officer had purchased an old country church for dismantling and had discovered that the rafters were made of solid walnut. From these antique boards he began turning out walnut frames to match the rough hewned country scenes of Smith's pen. Their proiect was so successful it assured Smith that he was on the right road to a new career.

This bit of success had an amazing effect not only on Smith, but on the forces which were reshaping his life. The Famous Artists Schools, noting his progress and the sacrifice he was making to obtain professional training, decided to grant him a paid-up scholarship. His counselor got the Shaeffer Pen Company in Fort Madison to furnish Smith with all the pens and colored inks needed to see him through the three year training program.

The counselor resolved to help Smith broaden his sensory experience, so that there would be more fuel to fire his artistic imagination. He knew that Smith went with his wife and three children every Sunday for a country drive but there just wasn't the time or opportunity to pause and make a quick sketch of scenes that could later be translated onto board or canvas. A good camera was needed. Thomas spread the word among a few persons in the community and suggested that a good camera might be obtained through trading stamps which are given with certain purchases. Within 48 hours the counselor was overwhelmed with more than enough to equip his client with a quality camera.

Word of Smith's unusual talent spread wide enough to be picked up by the Vernon Manufacturing Company in Newton. They sent a representative to see Smith, and after some discussion, offered him a hefty contract which commits him to draw 12 calendar pictures a year through the year 1970.

A new electric wheel chair (Everest & Jennings Standard Model) was another great step towards Smith's independence. He can now move around his home whenever he wishes. It also makes it a lot easier for him to work on his art assignments.

In an amazingly short time it now seems definite that Charles Lee Smith is on his way as an established artist. He has had two successful showings, one on the campus of Iowa State University at Ames and the other in a Des Moines department store. He has appeared twice on television. But most important, apart from his contract with the calendar company, he has sold 70 paintings to clinch his position as the family breadwinner once again, and to summon the respect of his neighbors, and to confirm his own confidence in himself.

It's a good feeling, also, to look up from a paralyzed position, and to think—not that the Iowa corn is tall . . . but that it's green.

o   o   o   o

Information and photos for this story courtesy of the President's Committee on Employment of the Handicapped and the Iowa Sickroom Supply Co., Des Moines.

Leathercraft For Beginners
John H. Banks

I started to title these suggestions "Leathercraft for the Handicapped Beginners." I cut the word handicapped because it was completely superfluous. All people are handicapped. No one is perfect. Their difference lies only in the area and the degree of handicap. From our first breath of life we begin to overcome our inherited handicaps, and later our imagined handicaps. To use the word handicap with the word beginners would be most assuredly superfluous because all beginners are automatically handicapped. They lack both confidence and knowledge. So speaking inversely any man that contains confidence and knowledge is certainly not handicapped. So I am writing these suggestions to all men and women that are beginners.

I think that leathercraft has fine attributes as either an avocation or a vocation. No matter which angle you approach it from you should confront it with the same attitude. Start with an enthusiastic and an open mind. A fine example to keep before your mind is children. Children are the real beginners. They are the beginners in life. They meet new problems every day. They meet them with a confident and positive mind. They enjoy, they practice, they study, and they imitate. And remember this, they ask for and accept help. They do not feel inferior or ashamed in so doing. Human beings like to help each other, and no man ever succeeded without the help of another.

I think the first step for a beginner is a talk with an established craftman. Tell him what you have in mind and I'm sure he will give you valuable help and suggestions. If you happen to be in any of the large towns where Tandy Leather Companies are located, I would suggest that you visit and talk to one of their managers. These managers are all leather experts. Most of the Tandy stores hold leather instruction classes. Almost all cities of any size have a civic organization that gives free lessons and instructions. If you happen to reside in a town where this service isn't available, I advise you to contact the Tandy Leather Company, Box 1386, Fort Worth, Texas.*

*New address: 2808 Shamrock, Fort Worth, TX 76107

Have them send you one of their catalogs and order a book called "Lucky Seven." This book costs $1.50 and is published by the Craftool Company of Los Angeles, California. In the "Lucky Seven" book you will find a list of beginners tools and primary instructions. A craftman must have good tools, but it is not advisable to obtain too many at first. Order the necessary tools and some scrap leather from the catalog. If you wish to deal with some company and you are not sure about the quality of their products contact the Chamber of Commerce or the Better Business Bureau for particulars.

After obtaining your tools, if you can't find an instructor don't give up. Sit down with your tools and your instruction book and read and practice. Your book will give you step-by-step photos to copy and practice by. I would suggest that you purchase a well carved and finished object. Study this as you practice as it will give you an idea

"No man ever succeeded without the help of another". John Banks shows his children the art of tooling.

toward what you are aiming. From here it is just a matter of reading all the books you can get and practice, practice, practice. I would also suggest that you take a subscription to "The Leather Craftsman" magazine. This magazine gives all the latest tips and innovations in leathercraft.

To you who are going to take up leather as a vocation. I would not try to carve the first leather projects that you intend to sell. There are many type leathers that don't have to be carved, and can be used to make various projects. There are also several companies that sell pre-carved projects and will pay a commission to salesmen. While you are practicing at home on your craft, you may start making a profit and building a clientele by selling plain projects and pre-carved projects. This will also help you with your craft because you will begin to learn the likes and dislikes of people in respect to leather. Deal fairly with yourself and with your customers and I'm sure you will be on your way to many happy and profitable hours.

Educational Film Producer

Some men are born physically disabled; others have physical disability thrust upon them. Thus it is today for 25 million physically handicapped Americans. I am one of these; a respiratory quadriplegic.

"Well, you're not going to die," the neurologist's words were matter-of-fact. "You have progressive muscular atrophy, a cousin to amyotrophic lateral sclerosis. You can expect another twelve to fifteen years of life."

As a registered physical therapist with fifteen years of clinical experience, I found his words familiar and yet distant. I had treated many types of neuromuscular disease and this diagnosis was no stranger. The impact it was to have on my life had not struck me with its full force. The changes, like the disease, would come slowly, progressively and relentlessly downward.

I had the luxury of time to endeavor to try to answer that question: "What do I do now?"

During my therapy years I tried to assist many patients to make the adjustment to disabling illness. I urged them to consider their future against the test of three basic questions:

1. What do I want to do?
2. What am I able to do?
3. What opportunities are available to me?

If my life had been based on these principles for others to follow, shouldn't I now apply the same criteria to my own case? And so, against the background of this trilogy of questions, I made my decision.

I did not want to give up my professional career as a physical therapist so the decision was made to try to continue that career through the media of educational motion picture production.

Since I practiced physical therapy in the center of the world's largest motion picture industry, Hollywood. I knew many skilled people in this industry so I turned to them with my idea. I had no formal training or experience in this new field. I did have the burning desire—the intense will to work. To me, to cease to work was the road to oblivion.

In 1963, together with a few friends, $600 in working capital and some ideas, Cinema Pictures, Inc. was incorporated under the laws of the State of California. The transition for me had begun.

Today, seven years later, Cinema Pictures, Inc. is completing its thirtieth production comprising twenty medical-educational films, one TV series of country-western music and eight theatrical short

Bob Dicus, with the help of his daughter Ann (at his left), discusses parts in new movie with starlets Kristie Pofgron and Denise Pauly.

subjects released through Paramount Pictures Corporation.

At this time, film production is almost exclusively devoted to telling the stories, the problems and the accomplishments of the physically disabled. This month we will complete the second in a series of advanced transfer techniques for quadriplegics for Rancho Los Amigos Hospital in Downey, California.

In this Republic we subscribe to the principle that effective change through government can best be accomplished by electing government officials who are responsive to the will of the people.

What is the will of the physically disabled? I do not know. I know what my will is. It is to be able to work, to contribute, to succeed or fail, to try and live as a free man; free from the pigeon holes of government, free from the tethers of voluntary health agencies, free from disease and disability. To have others in positions of government control, financial capability and motivated in a responsiveness to my will cannot be achieved by legislation alone.

The human potential is unlimited and usually untapped. We can accomplish many things whether we are physically disabled or not. We must begin by helping ourselves. It is only when I began to try to help myself that assistance was forthcoming. As long as I sat back and cried for help from government, that help never materialized.

The pride of life embodies not only the expectation of the right to an effective active life, but also the thirst to drink from that cup. If we, the physically disabled, are not thirsty enough to seek our own solutions for quenching our thirst, how can we expect others to be responsive to our will?

It has been said that this is the decade of the revolution of the handicapped. As a film maker, I see millions of untold stories of the great individual accomplishments of disabled people. Why not tell these stories to the world? Why not exploit the positive accomplishments and contributions of the misfits, failures, fugitives, outcasts and our like who are forced to grapple with the new and unknown? Perhaps in this way we can elicit a consensus of our will to which others can be responsive.

Bob and his wife Shirley often play chess to relieve the tension of demanding production schedules. He makes his move by using an electric arm activated by a mouth switch.

How To Start A Magazine Subscription Business In Your Home

Many a successful business has been started and handled from a living room. One of the easiest to start and maintain is your own magazine subscription business.

You are your own boss, you set your own working hours and your success depends upon how willing you are to work day after day and how much money you want to make.

A successful agent is one who offers his or her customers a service and handles the details in a business-like way. If you are interested in developing this type of business, you can write to any one or all of the following. They will send you more information along with their recommendations telling you how to start and what to do.

Allan Scott
The Reader's Digest
Pleasantville, New York

George H. Jones
Subscription Service Company
401-403 Tuscaloosa Avenue S. W.
Birmingham, Alabama

James T. Stewart
Box 281
Curtis Circulation Company
Independence Square
Philadelphia, Penna.

McGregor Magazine Agency
Department PL
Mount Morris, Illinois

A few hints that we think can be important in your success are:
1. Think of a good name for your business and have your own stationary printed (not too expensive). Much of your contact with people will be by mail and this is where they get their impressions whether or not you are the kind of person they want handling their subscription business. 2. Work on a selective basis, that is, instead of mailing out a great many letters and waiting for customers to come running (they won't), do mail out a friendly letter telling what you have to offer to only as many selected people that you can follow up in two or three days with a personal phone call.
3. Work on a "preferred lead" basis. Ask you first customers to give you the names of five friends who may appreciate your services. Mail these five your letter and then phone them two days later. Be sure to mention the name of the person who gave you their name.
4. Handle all business quickly. Get orders out the same day you get them if at all possible.
5. Work close with the agencies listed above. They are experts in the field.

Selling Gift Fruits

by Chris Ford

Villa Rose Citrus, P.O. Box 509, Sebring, Florida* is a new rehabilitation project offering a lucrative opportunity to responsible persons with cerebral palsy and other handicaps everywhere.

Our product, tree-ripened Florida citrus, has proved an overwhelmingly popular gift. What could be more welcome to you on one of those cold mornings, you are plagued with up North, than a gaily decorated basket of oranges, grapefruit and other citrus products? We offer more than a dozen specialty packages, each a colorful item of lasting usefulness.

Villa Rose has operated twelve years as a rehabilitation center for the cerebral palsied. It is located four miles south of Sebring in the heart of the Florida citrus belt. We the students are housed on a lakefront country estate, where we enjoy the benefit of Florida sunshine every day in the year. There have always been young adults on our roster, and we have given anxious thought to our vocational potentials. What could be more natural for a project than the fruit which grows so plentifully on our own trees, and is a highlight on our breakfast table each morning.

We have exhibited at State and County State Fairs. Our present efforts are largely concentrated on direct mail solicitation. Each Fall, we buckle down to our typewriters,

addressing and mailing brochures to a list which currently number 3,000. Miss Holly Shiffman, a graduate of the New York Institute for the crippled and Disabled in New York, is our very efficient full-time secretary.

Dealerships are available to reliable handicapped persons everywhere. Here is an opportunity to sell a product for which there is great demand, on a liberal scale. Our independent dealers supplement our efforts by conducting mail campaigns of their own. We figure a 50% commission after operating and express charges are deducted. The small remainder is used for promotion and to advance the program of Villa Rose, a nonprofit organization under the direction of Mrs. Rose C. McQuade. If you wish a dealership, write us a letter with your qualifications, and a sales kit will be made up for you.

Tree-ripened Florida citrus is the ideal gift for your friends, relatives, business associates, and especially shut-ins, at this holiday season, and through the winter months. A brochure and a list is available by return mail. Each time you purchase a box of VILLA ROSE CITRUS, you are helping the cerebral palsy help you, and enabling us in turn to give increased opportunity to others.

*New address is Rt. 2, Box 354, Sebring, FL 33870.

Selling Socks

Selling hosiery from her wheelchair, Pat Vardell has earned as high as $250 a month.

Mrs. Pat Vardell had polio in September, 1955, including 19 days in the iron lung.

She sells from her wheelchair in her home. Occasionally she invites friends over to acquaint them with her line of hosiery, but most of her business is done by phone. In her sales talk she tells them what she has and describes the colors and what they should be worn with. She explains the unusual guarantee and asks if they would like to try three pair and then asks them to send her a check. The order is then sent into the company and the order is delivered to the customer's home within a few days.

She has sold through various civic clubs, P.T.A.'s, notices on bulletin boards, notes delivered by paper boys, and of course, last but not least, word of mouth advertising.

She advises, "Of course, a person should have some education. The company does most of the figuring for you, but you have to know arithmetic and keep your wits about you when writing sales slips."

"At first I didn't think I liked the idea of selling, being rather timid, but it has been good for me and kept me in touch with friends I would never see in this busy city." Your success depends entirely on how much time you put into it, how many friends and contacts you have, and how much courage you have to go on calling people to find those who are interested."

My friends suggested selling magazines and Christmas cards, but those fields were crowded, so I prayed that something else would turn up. The next day I received a hosiery letter in the mail. It sounded so good I thought it was a racket of some sort and just about threw it away—but decided I would gamble the $10 on a sample kit which they promised would be repaid after I started selling. And it was! I will admit I had some doubts about the quality of the hosiery and the dependability of the company, but these were quickly dispelled. They put out a fine and beautiful line of hosiery and socks, including a guarantee on the wearing ability."

Selling Stamps
By Mail

Tad Tanaka chose the name Sierra Stamp Sales and started business in 1955 with a total capital outlay of $275, part of which was borrowed.

His advice to others interested in starting a business is, "You are no doubt fully aware that the successful establishment of a home business is not as simple as some

Life as a quadriplegic for stamp dealer Tad Tanaka began shortly after high school as the result of a mortorcycle-auto collision, resulting in the fracture of the cervical vertebra at the 7th level. He has partial use of his hands; his arms and shoulders were almost totally unaffected. Tad reflects, with a twinkle in his eye, "To be able to finally begin paying the cost of my vocational rehabilitation to the State in the form of taxes is, to be sure, deeply satisfying. It is also satisfying to be permitted the more or less universal privilege of singing the taxation blues".

borderline promoters would lead one to believe. It is easy enough to make or otherwise acquire the merchandise to sell, but the big trick is in marketing or selling, which problem, unhappily, one finds in the end is his alone to solve."

Tad, in his own words, explains how he did it.

"With current monthly sales running well over $600, perhaps my past experiences can now be viewed with certain amusement. The first year ended with only the barest hint of success potential. If anything was clear, it was that the situation called for a complete revision of my selling methods.

"The second phase began with great enthusiasm, but sad to say, only a very few months were needed to show that continuation without change would mean total depletion of funds and complete cancellation of this venture in stamps. Again I tried a totally revised method of selling.

"So began a third and final phase. Packaged sets of stamps to be sold to collectors on approval.

"Certainly a procedure familiar to almost every stamp collector, but this was not tried earlier due to well meaning advice from two wholesalers. To wit: too much work and too little money. Be that as it may, all this time and effort expended was not a complete loss. Advertising techniques, psychology of selling, awareness of trends, favorable buying sources; all were adding to my rapidly evolving pattern of overall direction.

"The years' total approval sales of $721.14 seems, to be sure, to be small . . . yet at that time, I felt that the future held much promise. Subsequent sales rose steadily and surely; when monthly sales reached $200, the Bureau of Vocational Rehabilitation helped out with two major pieces of equipment needed for my expanding business.

"Being a stamp collector, though not an absolute prerequisite for becoming a stamp dealer, would add immeasurably in making the selling of stamps a most interesting field. Many pamphlets and booklets on how to sell stamps include offers to sell you stamp selling kits. These should be read with some reservation. There is one book now on the market which is realistic in its approach to selling stamps and can be read just for entertainment, if not for profit. Stamp Dealing, by Lucius Jackson, 150 pgs., $3, can be secured from The Stamp Wholesaler, Burlington, Vermont.* This book gives it to you straight without the usual 'make lotsa money,

*Out of print. You may be able to obtain it from your public library.

very little work' routine. This book carefully explains the various procedures and if diligently studied should save much time and effort which would otherwise be required through trial and error. As you can tell from my earlier experiences, I did not have the advantage of reading this book when I was starting.

"In all fairness to those who might consider this business, perhaps it should be noted that one of the biggest obstacles is lack of sufficient capital. One can reasonably expect an annual sale of three times the total value of stock on hand. A small capital outlay will most likely require several years of work to compile an adequate working stock.

"If money is the only compensation desired, this is not the field to enter. If, however, one is challenged by competition and would like to meet it on equal terms, this would be ideal. You will, in effect, be competing with every other stamp dealer in the country since most of the stamps are sold through the mail and advertised in national magazines. In the normal course of business you will be approached by many dealers, not only in this country, but in countries abroad. As your volume increases it may be worthwhile to import stamps directly from the various national agencies.

"The variation of experiences in this field of dealing in stamps is virtually endless."

OTHER REFERENCES YOU CAN USE

Employment Opportunities for the Handicapped, Julian Angel, Simon & Schuster, 200 Park Ave. South, New York, N.Y. Lists some occupations, with what is required for equipment and skills, where employment is usually found and what disabilities pose no barrier to the performance of the job. Also lists some agencies in each state which could be of help in starting a business.

Employment for the Handicapped, Julietta K. Arthur, Abington Press, Nashville, Tenn. Devotes two chapters to starting one's own business and operating a business in the home. Also has bibliography and list of government offices specializing in employment. (Out of print. Check with your local public library.)

How to Get More Business by Telephone, Jack Schwartz, Jack Schwartz Telephone Sales Clinic, P.O. Box 24491, Village Station, Los Angeles, CA 90024. Points on courtesy, enunciation, salesmanship applicable to any business with a telephone.

How to Start and Operate a Mail-Order Business, Julian Simon, McGraw-Hill Book Co., 330 W. 42nd St., New York, N.Y. Detailed analysis of the business, includes advice on finding products, law, advertising and mailing methods.

Starting and Managing a Swap Shop or Consignment Sale Shop, Small Business Administration (SBA). Detailed instructions on such subjects as records, rules of the house, markdowns, customer relations, and where to get more information. Mostly for the shop-away-from-home, but could be applied to a home-based shop.

Starting and Managing a Small Duplicating And Mailing Service, SBA. General instructions for this business, easily adapted to the home. Technology of this type of business changes often, so technical information should be sought elsewhere.

Starting and Managing a Small Shoe Repair Service, SBA. Assumes working knowledge of shoe repair. Included are tips on setting up shop, keeping it going, stocking, advertising, displays and public relations.

Starting and Managing a Small Bookkeeping Service, SBA. Ground-level information for beginning the business. Assumes some knowledge of bookkeeping and accounting.

The Mother Earth News Handbook of Home Businesses, Mother Earth News staff, Bantam Books. Details of how to start and operate a business at home. Some ideas include: typing, garage sales, banking, upholstery, writing, lettering, and many others.

Woodworking Techniques for the Visually Handicapped Craftsman, Vocational Rehabilitation Administration and State University College, Oswego, N.Y. Useful woodworking patterns and instructions for easier construction by the blind.

accent on living magazine

- Brings you a unique kind of news and information, with strong emphasis on the practical day-to-day needs of individuals who have disabilities.

- Gives you a continuous source of new ideas and can serve as an important, valuable and time-saving reference for you.

- Is of special value to you because of the advertisements about a great variety of products, devices and services for the disabled.

accent on information

- A computerized retrieval system containing information to help persons with disabilities to live more effectively — with emphasis on products, assistive devices and how-to information.

accent special publications

- Provide you with practical reference material on specific subjects of interest to individuals who have a disability.

The services available through ACCENT On Living are provided especially for individuals who have a disability. Because much of the information comes from disabled people and has a high practical value the services of ACCENT are being utilized by professionals and students in rehabilitation as well as relatives and friends of those with disabilities.